- Dedicated to Granddaughter Hope Schulz

CONTENTS

PREFACE

I have taken the liberty of calling this book a letter. Readership is intended not only for parents but for teachers, every congressperson, every senator and the President of the United States. It's an attempt to convey to American parents, American educators, and national education policy makers the notion that since our country is first in the world in per-student educational expenditures, it is reasonable to expect that it should be first in the world in mathematics and science education.

From evidence gathered through meticulous research, I will show through specific instances and graphic illustrations that great progress is attainable if we modify our educational paradigm to align our mathematics and science curricula with international educational norms and practices.

There will be four parts to this letter. In part one—chapters one through seven—we will explore, through inquiry and analysis, the causes as to why American fifteen-year-old students are unable to compete with their international counterparts in both mathematics and science. We will look at why American students are inadequately prepared for university-level mathematics, the tool that is indispensable for understanding and research in science. Specific anomalies in our mathematics education curriculum will be identified, the ramifications will be laid out, and the solution, which currently exists in all other industrialized countries, will be proposed to fix the problem. In part two, there will be two chapters (eight and nine) specifying why the Common Core reform is regressive and ill-conceived, particularly for mathematics education. In chapter eight, we will delve into the details about the origin of Common Core: how it was conceived, designed, and implemented, as well as the specious nature of the personalities involved. We will look at the anomalies contained in the rollout, and the motives that spurred a hasty acceptance and implementation of the Common Core State Standards (CCSS) across the United States. We'll also look at why at least forty-two states and the District of Columbia are now stuck with this program that is frustrating for students, teachers, schools, school administrators, and school communities. In chapter nine, we'll focus on how the CCSS was accepted and promoted in one state, as an example of how it was implemented in others. In the process, we'll examine the questionable nature of the charter school/CCSS connections. Part three, chapter ten, consists of a number of suggestions, augmented by views of educational experts, as to what parents can do to improve the education of American children. Parents who engage in homeschooling should feel very well accommodated in this letter. Part four will be a general recapitulation of the issues and will include a discussion of some of the misconceptions about teachers and the teaching profession. Part five will be consistent with how letters are written and will contain a number of postscripts for clarification, accompanied by a set of enrichment explorations not only for parents but also for kindergarten through twelfth-grade teachers.

The consensus of the professional peers I've interviewed is that if this country takes the transformative steps suggested in this letter, our students will have the precollege readiness skills to achieve the same level of excellence in our universities as achieved by foreign-born students. I feel confident that if the proposed solution is implemented, historians will record that this was the critical moment when the United States came into its own as the world's powerhouse for education in mathematics, science, and engineering technology.

One more thing: The postscripts mentioned above consist of some simple and pleasurable activities, mostly in discrete mathematics, together with explanations of a number of simple concepts. I've also included some pedagogical strategies to help children build intuitive power through pattern observation. The ultimate goal is to have your children experience the joy and pleasure of mathematics, and this, in turn, will lead them to also enjoy explorations into the exciting and factual world of science.

ACKNOWLEDGMENTS AND THANKS

To my very capable editor Tad Martin. He was the answer to my quest for finding a skilled and experienced editor who also had knowledge of mathematics. I am extremely grateful for his patience, his advice, his tactical suggestions, his overall expertise, and his consummate professionalism. I have benefitted enormously from his services and have emerged with improved writing skills.

To Dr. Bruce Vogeli, Clifford Brewster Upton professor of mathematical education, Teachers College Columbia University, for recommending Tad Martin.

To Michael Schulz for the many times he promptly answered my call for help with graphics and shortcuts with the tools of Microsoft Word and for help with formatting issues.

To Susan Kanoff, my former colleague with parallel career paths. We were both mathematics teachers and served in supervisory roles as assistant principals of mathematics in the New York City School System as well as assistant professors at Passaic County Community College. She deserves gratitude for her constructive suggestions concerning the original draft of a paper out of which this book evolved. With content knowledge of mathematics and her pedagogical expertise, she offered the suggestions and critique that served as a practical guide to organizing and writing this book.

To Gina Wisdom-Perkins, English language arts teacher who was always there when I needed technical help in her area of expertise, and Matilda Lobban, for her useful suggestions after reading parts of the book.

Special thanks must be given to Matteo Michelotti for the internal design and formatting of this book to meet the standard requirements of the publisher. Thanks also to writer India Drummond (Matteo's wife) who recommended him to me.

Last but certainly not least, my dear wife, Vivienne, for her patience as well as her help in reading and making constructive suggestions as writing progressed, and to my awesome children Douglas and Claudia, who spurred me on with love and encouragement.

INTRODUCTION

When our country was founded, George Washington, our first president, submitted two transformative legislative proposals to the congress in the 1790s. One was to get rid of the complicated British currency and replace it with the simpler American dollar. The other was to get rid of the convoluted British system of measurements, "which itself evolved from a tangled mess of medieval weights and measures"[1] and replace it with the simpler metric system.[2] He succeeded with the first, but not the second. Later, another insightful president, James Madison, also suggested a complete change to the metric system, but he too was unsuccessful.[3] Today the magnitude of George Washington's foresight is manifested in the fact that the American dollar is the king of world currencies, but we continue to be intractably saddled with the archaic, medieval English system of measurements. Meanwhile, Great Britain itself has abandoned its own convoluted system and is now a metric system country. Here in the twenty-first century, the United States is the only industrialized country in the world not using the metric system exclusively. The consensus of many of my mathematics teacher colleagues is that the metric system is far more suited for mathematics and science than the US Customary System of measurements. Many of us believe that lack of use of the metric system is a prime contributing factor as to why fifteen-year-old American students have been lagging behind their counterparts on international tests. Furthermore, another possible serious consequence of using the old British system is that at critical times in the twentieth century, we have had to turn to foreign-born talents in mathematics, science, and engineering technology from metric system countries to assert and maintain our supremacy as a world power.

What really prompted the above retrospective and the writing of this book is the following statement: "If you made a list of countries around the world, with the best math scores, the United States would be on that list, in 25th place."[4] This is excerpted from an Exxon commercial that many Americans must have seen and heard on television. The same statement could have been made about the best science scores around the world, except that the United States would be in twenty-fourth place. These placement scores were the results of an international test given to fifteen-year-old students from fifty-seven participating countries, including the United States, in the year 2006. And yet this was neither the first nor the last time that the US scored disappointingly low in both subjects on that same test. This has been a consistent trend since the year 2000, when our country started participation in these triennial tests.[5]

There is another related problem that is serious for the future of the US. Companies and corporations needing employees for highly technical jobs involving mathematics, science, and engineering have experienced continuing difficulties finding sufficiently qualified Americans to fill such vacancies. At congressional hearings on immigration reform, large corporations such as Microsoft have stated these difficulties in emphatic terms. The following news item, by CNET, alluded to the serious nature of the issue:

> *For the second year in a row, Microsoft Chairman Bill*
> *Gates ventured to Capitol Hill and urged Congress to let*
> *more foreign-born engineers work in the United States*
> *and to direct larger numbers of tax dollars to research and*
> *education.*[6]

The congressional hearings attended by Bill Gates were intended to influence immigration reform legislation. Unfortunately, the term "immigration reform" means different things to different people. For US companies, the need for qualified applicants to fill highly technical job vacancies, for which they cannot find sufficient American candidates, impels them to seek reform or modification of our current laws to allow recruitment of candidates from other countries. In particular, they have requested that foreign-born graduate students who complete university degrees in the US be incentivized to legally stay in this country, rather than return to their homelands.

It is worthy of note that most of these students have high school preparation, or what we would call K–12 education, in their home countries, and they are admitted to our universities with all the precollege academic readiness skills. As such, they come fully prepared to start studies at higher subject levels than their US counterparts. As university graduates with superior grade point averages, they become prime candidates for recruitment to fill job vacancies in mathematics, in science, and in engineering.

Putting all this together, all pointers have indicated that American students completing K–12 education have fallen lamentably short in precollege preparation, particularly in the subject disciplines of mathematics and science. Indications from reliable data make it clear beyond doubt that something significant is lacking in the way we prepare our students for university degrees in these two subjects.

A look at educational reform initiatives since the year 2000 will show that this country's leadership has been aware of the inherent educational deficiencies, and specific steps have been taken to address them. There have been a number of presidential initiatives focusing specifically on mathematics and science education, but since the most recent international tests scores show no improvements, it leaves no doubt that all such efforts were palpably ineffective.

The Obama administration's "Race to the Top" plan has engendered a number of programs such as the Science, Technology, Engineering, and Mathematics (STEM) initiative. Unfortunately, the majority of American students passing through our K–12 system will never participate in the likes of the STEM program, because of its limits in scope and availability. No previous initiatives, nor those under the "Race to the Top" umbrella, have focused on the adoptable and translatable elements utilized by the international community that would facilitate an early childhood start in mathematics and science for every student in the US. Instead, there is an overarching tendency, particularly by politicians, to shower praise on the few programs that succeed by selecting specially gifted students, while placing blame on teacher quality and on schools when the majority of students fail to show improvements. This has led to a 2009 quid pro quo between states and the federal government stipulating that in order to receive federal funding, states must agree to certain conditions. In one significant case, states had to agree to create more privately managed charter schools, at the expense of the public school system.

The most recent and the most controversial of the "Race to the Top" derivatives, the one containing the charter schools quid pro quo, is the Common Core State Standards (CCSS). It includes a number of questionable curriculum modifications accompanied by punitive measures for schools and school personnel, a situation that was not well received by professional educators. Parents, teachers, students, school administrators, and state governors who originally envisioned the CCSS as a constructive reform initiative have discovered, to their dismay, that it is awfully regressive and destructive.

It appears that the CCSS was able to move into a vacuum that exists in the way we educate our children in the K–12 system. History has recorded the existence of educational vacuums at crucial times in the previous century.

One of the most serious educational voids with national-interest implications occurred on October 4, 1957. The Soviet Union, dominated by Russia, shocked the United States with the launching of Sputnik, the first man-made space satellite, into orbit around the Earth. This stunning event and its ramifications, recorded in a book entitled *Sputnik: Shock of the Century*,[7] brought into stark relief the extent and magnitude of the existing deficiencies in American technology. It impelled us to conclude that there were serious curriculum shortcomings in our educational system, particularly in mathematics and science.

Alarmed by the challenge posed by Sputnik, the United States responded by setting out to harness available national engineering resources, but the magnitude of the educational void was so great that there was no alternative but to turn to foreign-educated scientists to fill the gap. In 1960, the newly formed National Aeronautics and Space Administration (NASA) enlisted a German scientist who was skilled in rocket-propulsion technology to head its rocket program.[8] The following description of that scientist is taken from the "Encyclopedia Astronautica":

> *von Braun, Wernher* (1912–1977) *German-American chief designer, leader of the 'Rocket Team'; developed the V-2, Redstone, Jupiter, and the Saturn rockets that took US to the moon. He made the idea of space travel popular in the 1950's and a reality in the 1960's.*[9]

Dr. Wernher von Braun was a German-educated rocket scientist who received his PhD at age twenty-two. He was the leader in the creation of the V-2 rocket, a weapon that the Germans used in World War II to devastate parts of Great Britain in 1944.[10] Skepticism about the future of his home country led him to arrange the surrender of himself and 500 other German scientists to the Americans before the end of World War II.[11]

With this extraordinary collection of foreign-born scientists, over the next four decades the US was able to utilize the available rocket propulsion knowledge base to successfully answer the Sputnik challenge. This was actualized through the launching of all kinds of satellites, highlighted by an American landing on the moon in 1969, followed by several follow-up missions to Earth's natural satellite. Subsequently, we sent exploratory missions to the planet Mars. We have also launched the Hubble space telescope and sent several spacecraft on missions to explore the solar system and interstellar space. Most of our current media communication and navigation systems are possible because of evolving satellite technology and improved rocket propulsion. We participated in the creation and the activities of the International Space Station with back-and-forth travel using our own space shuttle vehicles. The miniaturization of the central processing unit in computers, leading to the ubiquity of the computer chip in various technological devices, became possible because of the technical demands of the space program.

These are monumental scientific achievements for our country, which began with the shock of Sputnik. But we proceed with great peril if we forget that our post-Sputnik achievements were attained by utilization of foreign-born scientific intellectual resources. Wernher von Braun and most of the 500 German scientists have passed on. And so those technological skills that sparked a revolution in American technology appear to be on the wane, and we are losing momentum and dominance. Indeed, our universities have been turning out American scientists, mathematicians, and engineers, but not in sufficient quantities to meet technological demands. Ominous signs of stagnation if not decline are on the horizon. For example, the space shuttle program was phased out before building its replacement, and now we depend on the Russians for taking our astronauts to the International Space Station. In 2014, the United States paid the Russians $457 million for such services.[12] In 2015, the cost went up to $490 million.[13] Back in November 2014, we learned of the awesome technological and engineering feat of the successful landing of the spacecraft Philae on a comet in deep space. But Americans can only watch and applaud this amazing success story from the sidelines, because the Philae spacecraft (which landed on the comet) was a product of the Rosetta Space probe launched by the European Space Agency.

When we look at the facts, we are less dominant in space exploration, we cannot find Americans in sufficient quantities to fill job vacancies in technology, and our students at age fifteen are being dramatically outperformed by their international counterparts in mathematics and science. We do not have the now defunct Soviet Union to contend with, but this is no different than a Sputnik moment in time. Our international placement in science and mathematics literacy indicates that we have an endemic educational crisis in these two subjects. The fact that American fifteen-year-old students cannot score inside the top ten on the list of participating countries, particularly with the money we spend per student, should be so shocking and alarming that we should be demanding immediate national action to address this urgent issue.

We must begin at the preschool level to foster the environment that can produce engineers and scientists such as the likes of Wernher von Braun and his cohort of 500 scientists. Strong evidence will be presented in this letter, showing that the highly qualified foreign-born scientists and engineers we have been importing and seek to continue to import, as well as foreign-born scientists whose theories we have utilized, all came from a **metric system** environment. Wernher Von Braun and his 500 fellow scientists are not the only metric system scientists that have made significant contributions to American technological advances. Years before the Sputnik event, there were lessons to be learned from World War II. Victory over the Japanese in that war was achieved by the design, creation, and deployment of the atomic bomb, through the venture known as the Manhattan Project, an undertaking that consisted of a team dominated by foreign-born scientists, all of whom were educated in countries employing the metric system.

Before World War II, it was Nobel Laureate Niels Bohr, a theoretical physicist from Denmark, who created the atomic theory that facilitated the splitting of the atom by German scientists. It was Werner Heisenberg of Germany, another Nobel Laureate, who created quantum mechanics, the mathematics of the interior world of the atom that facilitated the calculations needed for success in the Manhattan Project. During World War II, it was German-born scientist Albert Einstein and Hungarian physicist Leo Szilard who composed a letter alerting President Roosevelt that German scientists had succeeded in splitting the atom. Three of the lead physicists in the Manhattan Project were born and educated in a metric system environment. Enrico Fermi was Italian born, and Edward Teller and Leo Szilard were Hungarian born.[14] After World War II, Edward Teller was instrumental in the design and creation of the hydrogen bomb, an invention that replicates the functioning processes of the sun, where hydrogen is fused to form helium. It is for this reason that Teller was called "the father of the hydrogen bomb."[15]

Speaking of bombs, since the 1990s the US has been highly successful in using laser-guided bombs to destroy enemy targets. The most reliable workhorse in the delivery of these bombs on target is the

B2 Stealth Bomber, a so-called "flying wing." Here is a description of the aircraft by Northrop-Grumman:

> *The U.S. Air Force's B-2 stealth bomber is a key component of the nation's long-range strike arsenal, and one of the most survivable aircraft in the world. Its unique capabilities, including its stealth characteristics, allow it to penetrate the most sophisticated enemy defenses, and hold at risk high value, heavily defended targets. The B-2 has demonstrated its capabilities in several combat scenarios, including Operation Allied Force in Kosovo, Operation Enduring Freedom in Afghanistan, Operation Iraqi Freedom, and most recently, in Libya, during Operation Odyssey Dawn.*[16]

While we are fortunate to have this effective offensive as well as defensive weapon in our military arsenal, we must be reminded of two facts. First, the architectural conception of a bomber in the form of a "flying wing" originated with Germany.[17] Second, the key aspect of the bomber, the stealth technology that makes it virtually invisible to radar, was developed by a Russian physicist. According to *Defence-aerospace.com*:

> *The history of stealth technology began in 1966, when radar specialists at Lockheed came across an article written by physicist Peter Ufimtsev in a popular Soviet scientific and technical journal. The article said that a certain type of aircraft made of particular materials and with a specific angular shape and paint could be almost invisible to radar. This article piqued the interest of American military experts, who decided to build and test such an aircraft.*[18]

The emergence of all these technologies that originated with foreign talent took place in the 1900s. But how are we doing in the twenty-first century? Well, in 2014 the Nobel Prize for Physics went to three Japanese-born physicists. *The New York Times* published the misleading headline, "2 Japanese, and 1 American Share Nobel Prize in

Physics for work on LED Lights."[19] But don't be fooled into thinking that the "American" was American born. In effect the statement is true, but it is misleading in its implication. The two Japanese named were Isamu Akasaki and Hiroshi Amano and the American was Shuji Nakamura. The fact is that all three physicists were born and educated in Japan, but Shuji Nakamura is an immigrant who is now a naturalized American citizen. The Times headline correctly claimed Nakamura as American, but did not highlight that he was Japanese born and educated.

What do all these accomplished, foreign-born, foreign-educated scientists and Nobel Prize winners have in common? As previously indicated, and it is important to emphasize, they were all—every single one of them—educated in countries that had a **metric system** environment.

For over thirty-five years, we have tried several American-based ideas to address existing deficiencies in mathematics and science education, and nothing seems to work. The latest of these ideas is the Common Core State Standards (CCSS). Professional educators see this program as spurious, because before it was imposed across the country, it was *accepted before it was completed!* Because of the rush to implement the CCSS, it was neither field-tested nor piloted, and therefore had no empirical underpinnings. Intricate analysis of the program found educationally pernicious issues, such as teacher evaluation standards based on test scores from tests made up by publishing houses, threat of school closings, and convoluted class and homework assignments, together with inaccurate editing—all of which created collective confusion in and out of the classroom. Reports from communities and school districts suggest that the CCSS does very little to advance mathematics and science education, and an argument can be made that it is regressive. The lead writer for the CCSS mathematics has admitted that the standards for the subject represent a deliberately truncated curriculum, "with fewer topics in each grade."[20] Was the reduction in the number of concepts in the CCSS K–12 mathematics curriculum due to the hurried nature of its construction? On the other hand, it does a lot to terrify teachers, students, and parents, while simultaneously advancing the prospects of creating more privately managed charter schools. It is apparent that the CCSS was constructed by opportunistic individuals who were more motivated to exploit the availability of over $5 billion in federal funds than to seriously address the real issues affecting curriculum constructs and the delivery of mathematics instruction in this country.

Meanwhile, the urgency to fix our current problem cannot be overstated. The good news is that practical modalities are available and can easily be phased in to effectuate a permanent fix. It has to do with providing the appropriate environment, as other countries do, for our children's preschool enculturation, to prepare and enable them to acquire optimum K–12 precollege education, particularly with mathematics and science. High competence levels in these two subjects are necessary to achieve the goal of maintaining an America that is second to none in the word. I believe we can harness the same effort that characterized our reaction to the launch of Sputnik.

It is instructive to look at how the US Congress reacted when the Russian satellite was launched. "One result of Sputnik was that Congress passed a bill to increase math and science education in US schools. This was passed to prompt future scientists for the burgeoning weapon industry."[21] Not only that, a special new government agency, National Aeronautics and Space Administration (NASA), was created and signed into law by President Eisenhower, as described in the following statement:

> In 1958, Eisenhower signed a bill to create NASA. Other initiatives were passed into law to promote math, science, engineering, and project management. To this day, many educational programs are still in place that were begun during the arms race.[22]

It is evident that those educational programs that are "still in place" will need continuing upgrading. In the 1950s and the 1960s, we had an enlightened Congress that took appropriate actions to address crises that had national-interest implications. The legacy of Congress in those days is one that Americans can savor with satisfaction, with pride, and with delight. Today's unenlightened Congress seems more concerned about the interests of lobbyists and religious issues than it does for the national interest. Arbitrariness, capriciousness, lack of foresight, and being not the least concerned about wasting the taxpayers' money constitute the modus operandi of today's Congress when it comes to educational and research issues. It was a relatively recent Congress that passed legislation to end support for an American-built particle accelerator and supercollider that may have discovered the Higgs boson. First the congress supported funding for the project, as attested to by the following statement:

> In the mid 1980s, the United States wanted to construct the largest particle collider in the world. What was to be called the Superconducting Super Collider (SSC) began as an idea in 1983. By 1987 Congress had approved the $4.4 billion dollar budget for the project, and by 1991 a site had been chosen in Texas and construction began.[23]

After construction began, and over $2 billion was spent, there was a deficit debate in the Congress and the funding for the project was summarily discontinued. According to *The Baltimore Sun*:

> The abrupt cut-off in funding for the $11 billion Superconducting Supercollider project last November represented a victory for congressional deficit hawks, but it left the future of particle-physics research in this country in limbo. The short-term effect has been to cede U.S. leadership on one of the cutting edges of modern science.[24]

The United States wasted $2 billion on infrastructure that is now defunct, and ceded the supercollider to overseas interests. This resulted in the construction of the Large Hadron Collider (LHC) at Cern, Switzerland. It was at the LHC that the long-sought-after subatomic particle, the Higgs boson, was discovered, instead of in Texas. Here is the reaction of Trevor Quirk in *Texas Monthly*:

> The Higgs boson, a particle that has shaped the theories of modern particle physics, was discovered at a super collider in

Geneva. It was a hugely significant moment for Big Science, one that received a Nobel Prize earlier this year — and it should have been discovered in Texas.[25]

A case in point in comparing today's US Congress to its predecessors is that the Congress of the 1960s discovered that there was one significant change in the area of science and mathematics that was omitted in the 1950s, and sought to correct it. In 1968, it took steps to address the issue. It had to do with changing our measurement systems from the US Customary System (USCS) to the metric system. This was a moment of great promise, because of the proven history of the value-added asset that is the metric system, particularly for science and mathematics education. After a study and a report by the Department of Commerce, the US Congress took action and passed a truncated measure called the "The Metric Act of 1975."[26]

In pages ahead, the point will be made that if that legislation had been passed with inclusion of all of its original recommendations, today's American students would be as competent in mathematics and science as their international counterparts. With the money spent per pupil on education, our students' performance would be at least in the top ten countries, if not number one in the world. As for the technology job market, we would be hiring highly qualified and skilled Americans to fill job vacancies requiring proficiency in mathematics, science, and engineering technology, instead of having the need to hire foreign-born talents. But now, that singular short-sighted congressional exclusion has resulted in the educational consequences we are grappling with today. In short, we had our opportunities to do the productive thing as a country, but we missed it, and as the saying goes, "the chickens are coming home to roost."

Our country has become inured to the USCS, and that, as it will be demonstrated, is the main reason our students are not competitive in mathematics and science. The USCS will continue to be an obstruction to producing a sufficient number of great scientists and for the US to obviate the need to hire foreign talent. Let's not deceive ourselves about the USCS just because there have been a few American-born Nobel Prize winners in the sciences. For example, Nobel Prize–winning physicists Robert Oppenheimer and Richard Feynman, who both worked on the Manhattan Project, were American born, but they were exceptional students with foreign backgrounds. Richard Feynman, for example, was exceptionally gifted. He taught himself elementary-school mathematics before entering elementary school, and on his own, he completed high-school mathematics and more, and he was ready to enter university at age fifteen.[27] Feynman and Oppenheimer had one thing in common that shielded them from the ravages of the USCS. They were both children of immigrant parents who came from metric system countries. Feynman's parents were from Belarus, and Oppenheimer's were from Germany. In chapter 2, we will learn that Germany has been on the metric system since 1872. Italy, Enrico Fermi's country of birth, converted in 1863. Hungary, the country of birth of Leo Szilard and Edward Teller, went on the metric system in 1876. Japan, the country of birth of the three 2014 Nobel Prize winners in Physics, went on the metric system in 1957.

It is safe to say that most if not all foreign students who come to seek university degrees in mathematics, science, and engineering technology in the US—the ones Bill Gates et al. are proposing to encourage to stay in this country—had precollege preparation in a metric system environment.

The purpose of this letter to the parents of America is to provide persuasive evidence that the nation will have an increased number of well-prepared students at the precollege level only after we implement the **metric system** (MS) for both commerce and education in the United States. Our students will become the graduates we seek to hire, and we can become less dependent on foreign-born personnel for jobs requiring skills in mathematics, science, and engineering technology. In the chapters ahead, particularly chapters 5, 6, and 7, I will show conclusively why the MS is superior to the USCS. The progressive elements of the MS for mathematics and science education will be graphically illustrated. In like manner, the regressive elements of the USCS will be demonstrably portrayed.

I'm writing as one who has had experiential knowledge as a mathematics educator in this country for over thirty years. I have been a mathematics teacher at the middle school, high school, and college levels.[28] I have structured the letter to give factual information from sources and individuals with expertise in the field of education in general, and in mathematics and science in particular.

In advocating the merits of the metric system, particular consideration will be given to parents who home-school their children. I will discuss, in layman's language, the basic concepts of mathematics, of which mastery is required in the K–12 curriculum. Since we must begin in elementary school for effect, there will be a focus on elementary school mathematical concepts, along with concepts that are at the intersection of mathematics and science. My goal is to acquaint parents with proven methodologies that have been utilized to achieve optimum precollege preparation. I will demonstrate clearly how this can be accomplished right here in the US.

In giving consideration to homeschool instruction, it must be stated that I consider all parents as homeschool educators. If your child is educated exclusively at home, then you are a full-time homeschool educator. If your child is educated at school, then you are a part-time homeschool educator; in order for your child to have optimal success, you must be an active participant in the affairs of your school district, you must monitor your child's homework assignments, and you must engage your child in extracurricular activities that can be enjoyable, while enhancing the learning process.

In chapter 10, I've included a number of activities and suggestions as to how you, as parents, can augment and enrich the learning process by consciously engaging your youngsters outside of classroom time. I will be reviewing, in a value-added manner, some of the underlying mathematics concepts that the average parent studied in elementary school, so that you can offer positive help to your youngsters. I will also demonstrate how measurement systems can impact how children learn the fundamentals of mathematics and science.

I'm also writing with the contingency that today's US Congress may refuse to change measurement systems. The task ahead is formidable but not impossible. But, to reiterate, there are actions and steps you can take in your capacity as parents to influence politics to improve the education of all America's children in science and mathematics. Some Americans may be able to influence one student at a time; others one school district at a time; others one state at a time; and before you know it, you can have influence on the whole country.

As an educator, I have seen parental power at work. Involved parents can do monumental things to make certain that children get the best education available in our country. It is my aim that at the conclusion of this letter, you will have a clear view as to the nature of the problem in the US, and that you will be able to formulate ideas as to the part you can play in the solution.

PART I

THE PROBLEM AND THE SOLUTION

CHAPTER 1:
Bad News for Mathematics and Science Education in the United States

It was announced in September 2013 that **US students placed thirtieth in the world in mathematics and twenty-third in science on an international test**. These disappointing results inform us about the performance of American fifteen-year-old students on a test given by the Programme for International Student Assessment (PISA) in 2012. The PISA test, which is given to this age group in fifty-seven countries, was designed and implemented by the Organization of Economic Co-operation and Development (OECD) to test competence levels in these two disciplines, as well as in reading literacy, and has been given every three years since 2000. Thus the United States was a participant in 2003, in 2006, in 2009, and in 2012.[29]

There have been several media comments and questions about these recent alarming results. I've selected one report that pinpoints the issue on a time-interval comparison basis. According to Valerie Strauss of the *Washington Post*, the US National Center for Educational Statistics (NCES) issued the following statements: "The U.S. mathematics literacy average score in 2012 was not measurably different than any earlier comparable time point (2003, 2006 and 2009)."[30] As for performance in science: "The U.S. science literacy average score in 2012 was not measurably different than either earlier comparable time point (2006 and 2009)."[31] Considering the fact, stated by the OECD, that **the United States spends more money per student on education than any other country in the world,**[32] these results are stunningly disappointing and should be unacceptable to taxpayers and parents alike.

The problem of precollege preparation deficiencies and the low performance of American students in mathematics and science when compared to their international counterparts has been a long-standing issue on record and has been a national concern for over thirty-five years. In 2006 the following statement was issued by the National Science Foundation:

> *Nearly a quarter century ago, the National Science Board's Commission on Precollege Education in Mathematics, Science and Technology assessed the state of U.S. precollege education in the subject fields and found it wanting. In the intervening years, we have failed to raise the achievement of U.S. students commensurate with the goal articulated by that Commission—that U.S. precollege achievement should be "best in the world by 1995"—and many other countries have surpassed us. Not only are they not first, but by the time they reach their senior year, even the most advanced U.S. students perform at or near the bottom on international assessments. There is now an even more pressing need to build a new foundation. The Science and Engineering Indicators 2006 report clearly describes the extent of the dilemma; the time to act is now!*[33]

As can be observed, the problem was recognized, assessment was made, and a goal was set to make the United States "best in the world" in precollege achievement in mathematics and science by 1995. Take note of the urgency expressed in that last sentence: "the time to act is now!" That "now" was in 2006, long past the 1995 time point, and yet in spite of the ongoing explicit imperative to act, we have these dreadful PISA results in 2012.

Over the past fifteen years, the issue of how to improve mathematics and science education has been taken seriously by our government at the Federal and state levels, and by the private sector.

We have had presidential initiatives such as "No Child Left Behind" (NCLB), associated with President George W. Bush, but after implementation, it was viewed by several educational professionals as a paradigm shift that encouraged "teaching to the test." Teaching to the test utilizes a "how-to" paradigm in problem solving. It does not deal with the "why this or why that," and so the set of keys to the underlying concepts that would build a solid foundational base in a subject area such as mathematics is intrinsically compromised. A test, particularly in mathematics, is a measure or indicator of the acquisition and application of key concepts in a course of study. Teaching to the test amounts to studying only the synopsis or skeleton in the outline of course concepts, without the fullness and contextual elements of the broader body of knowledge that make up the content of a course of study. NCLB had no specific focus or particular intent to address mathematics and science education. However, after the disappointing 2006 PISA results, there was a robust presidential response by the same Bush administration with a focus on helping American students to succeed in algebra. The succeeding Obama administration took action when the 2009 PISA results showed no improvement over past performances. The imperative to act led to the promulgation of a number of initiatives under the generative name "Race to the Top." This in turn led to proposals such as the Science, Technology, Engineering, and Mathematics (STEM) program. Then in 2010 there was a rollout of the very controversial Common Core State Standards (CCSS), which this letter will address later.

In addition to governmental initiatives, large companies such as Exxon, Chevron, Microsoft, and Dell have been making significant contributions to improve mathematics and science education. They have different approaches, but the goal is the same. Exxon has created initiatives to improve the teaching of mathematics and science in general, while Chevron, the Bill and Melinda Gates Foundation, and the Michael and Susan Dell Foundation have made significant contributions to the STEM program.[34] The problem is that special programs such as STEM, while very effective for a selected set of students, are limited in scope and do not extend to the entire student populace nationwide.

1.1 *Appropriate Questions for Concerned Parents*

With several well-intended efforts in place, the unchanging situation reflected in the low placements on the PISA tests has prompted many questions from parents or caregivers of children, for the media, and for a concerned citizenry. Considering the comparative magnitude of this country's per-student expenditure when compared to all other countries, why are we not getting a commensurate educational bang for the buck? Why, are American fifteen-year-old students being continually outperformed by their international counterparts? Will the next and future PISA tests show improved results based on past or current initiatives? Due to the persistence and seeming intractability of the problem, are we missing something? Are there adoptable norms in the competing international environment that have been overlooked or ignored—norms that we could implement in this country, that would enhance the ability of our children to make significant improvements? If there are existing models or systems that have empirical impact on mathematics education, could we amalgamate them into our educational culture, with the goal to at least move the United States into the top ten among the OECD countries involved in the PISA test?

We don't have to look very far for answers. For example, Canada, our contiguous neighbor country north of the US border, has never dropped below the top ten, neither in mathematics nor in science. Do Canada and the countries that consistently outperform the United States have a common supportive resource in their educational systems that is lacking in this country? On the obverse side of the issue, are there replaceable elements in our educational, economic, or commercial systems that can be modified or completely changed to bring about improvement in mathematics and science education? Would such modifications cause undue material or psychological inconvenience for Americans?

When a problem is misunderstood, flawed analysis is inevitable. This in turn leads to flawed solutions. Within the decade of 2000 to 2010, we have had multiple sets of analyses, all followed by plausible-sounding solutions. If the 2012 PISA results are a measure of the effectiveness of such solutions, then there is no other conclusion than that the money that was spent—and we are talking billions and billions of dollars—was an arbitrary and egregious waste of taxpayers' money. The sad part is that many of these programs were sold to us as definitive solutions, and yet, as the results have shown, they did very little to address the issue. We are the United States of America. We spend more money per student than any other country in the world. There must be something we can do to improve our students' performance in science and mathematics.

The most recent, perhaps the most far-reaching, and certainly the most controversial of the reform initiatives, is the new and current Common Core State Standards (CCSS). We are told by advocates such as Secretary of Education Arne Duncan and the so-called "national advocate of the Common Core Standards," the then commissioner of education in New York, John B. King Jr., that the CCSS is the definitive solution for mathematics and science. To give credence to their affirmation, they have stipulated conditions that include evaluation of teachers, schools, principals, and other school staff with punitive consequences if students fail to reach certain benchmarks based on tests scores. As stated before, we will discuss the general characteristics of the CCSS in chapters 8 and 9.

CHAPTER 2:
Inquiry and Discovery—
The Key to the Solution of
the Problem

The next generation of American students must be of paramount concern to all of us. If we can fix the math/science problem and make our educational expenditure commensurate with results, the generations that follow will reap the benefits, and our country will be second to none. Our country's placement of thirtieth in the world in mathematics should be so unacceptable that it should spur an immediate national call for action.

To say we have a huge problem is an understatement. According to the eminent mathematician George Polya, you cannot solve a problem if you don't understand it. It is clear, from the 2012 results, that the people responsible for all the previous and current initiatives designed to fix the problem had little or no understanding of the problem. American children are continuously being shortchanged and treated as unproductive guinea pigs in all kinds of untested unempirical schemes, in an environment that is perpetually regressive for mathematics and science education. Meanwhile, the money we spend seems to disappear, as if it went over the event horizon of a black hole.

I have looked at the specifics of the problem through the lens of a mathematics teacher as well as through external sources. I've consulted colleagues who, like me, have lived through myriads of untested and unpiloted educational changes and impositions, only to see them abandoned, leaving generations of children victims in the disastrous wasteland of failed initiatives. I have checked with mathematics teacher colleagues around this country, and I have also interviewed persons who have been educated in countries such as Russia, Canada, and South Africa to determine why fifteen-year-old US students are continually being outperformed in mathematics and science by their international counterparts.

For over thirty-five years in this country, I have been engaged in the educational hierarchy through the process of being a middle school teacher, a high school teacher, a supervisor of teachers of mathematics, a mathematics teacher trainer, an evaluator of high school mathematics teachers, a mathematical pedagogical consultant at the college level, and a tenured mathematics professor at a community college in the United States. I have had long memberships in the National Council of Teachers of Mathematics (NTCM) and the Mathematics Association of America (MAA). It is from this perspective and from the consensus of mathematics teacher colleagues that I can share with you what I'm convinced is the real cause of the problem, and more importantly, what I'm convinced is the real solution.

2.1 Comparing the United States with other OECD Countries

I first became aware of the Program for International Student Assessment (PISA) test in the year 2003, when the United States placed twenty-eighth in the world in mathematics. As a mathematics teacher and an American, I was shocked. The only apt description of the dimensions of my thought is a paraphrase of the words of Winston Churchill. It was like a puzzle wrapped in a mystery inside an enigma.

Since then, I have given considerable thought to the problem. After the 2009 results, when the US placement was not significantly different from previous results, I felt I had a professional duty and the responsibility as a citizen to do or say something. After analysis, I developed a conjecture detailing a solution to the problem. I wrote a paper on the matter. It was copyrighted in 2011, but it was unpublished. I mailed a copy to Secretary of Education Arne Duncan but got no reply. After being informed of the 2012 results, in which the United States placed thirtieth in mathematics and twenty-fourth in science, I decided it was time to act, and so I started this inquiry anew. For reasons that will become clear later, I began by looking back at the data of the PISA test results in 2006, as seen in the PISA ranking chart, figure 2.1 below. The chart shows that the United States placed twenty-fifth in mathematics and twenty-fourth in science on the PISA test given that year.

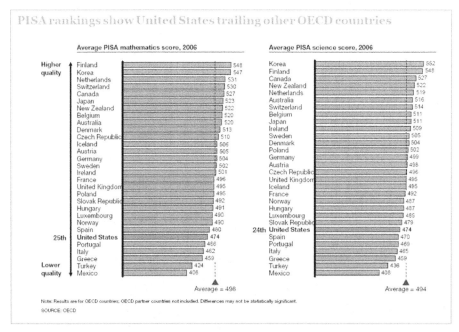

Figure 2.1: *Source: http://www.intellectualtakeout.org/library/chart-graph/pisa-rankings*

When 2006 PISA placements in mathematics and science are compared with the latest placements in 2012, where we respectively placed thirtieth and twenty-third in the world, it shows that in six years we are trending down in mathematics, while remaining relatively static at low and unacceptable performance levels in science.

Further inquiry led me to two significant pieces of information. First, in response to the 2006 PISA results, President George W. Bush created the National Mathematics Advisory Panel (NMAP). The panel was formed "to advise the President and the Secretary of Education on the best use of scientifically based research to advance the teaching and learning of mathematics."[35] It was charged "with making recommendations on improving mathematics achievement for all students, with a focus on preparing students to take and succeed in algebra."[36] It will be shown later that an early start in algebra is the key to excellence in mathematics. Algebra sets the students on a progressive path, taking them from discrete mathematics on to continuous mathematics. Knowledge of continuous mathematics is indispensible for science and engineering.

Armed with its mission, the NMAP went to work, and after reviewing over 1,600 research documents and reports, the panel issued its own final report, entitled "Foundations for Success,"[37] in March 2008. It is particularly important to note that on page 9 of the report, a survey of teacher input by the National Opinion Research Center at the University of Chicago had the information that one of the mathematics teacher responses cited was a need for "More focus on **positive vs. negative numbers**," among other basic concepts, such as fractions and decimals.[38] This emphasis on "**negative vs. positive numbers**" will be an **idée fixe** throughout this letter.

The NMAP report targeted five broad areas of findings but left out emphasis on the key to success in algebra, which is the issue of knowledge of negative vs. positive numbers, as suggested by mathematics teacher input. Thus the mission of the charge assigned to the NMAP, the "focus on algebra," was immediately compromised, because it missed the most important foundational element for students: to succeed in algebra. As will be demonstrated later, this is the key to start algebra in much earlier grades than is the current practice in the United States.

It was also obvious that the panel took an insular approach in that it failed to recognize international norms regarding measurement systems and their relations to mathematics and science education. The results of the 2012 PISA test in mathematics, when compared with the 2006 results, is a specific testament that the recommendations of the NMAP report had no progressive effect at best, and at worst it was regressive. Here is a case where several very smart people were engaged,[39] lots of money and time were expended on research involving over 1,600 documents, and yet we have nothing but regression to show for it.

In the second item of significance, the CIA reported in 2006 that all countries except the United States, Liberia, and Myanmar utilize the metric system of measurement. In addition, the United States, Belize, and Jamaica were the only three countries in the world that continued to use the Fahrenheit scale.[40] It should be stated, parenthetically, that Jamaica went metric in 1998, but in 2006 the Celsius scale was still in a phase-in stage, where television, radio stations, and media outlets reported temperatures in both scales.

Was the 2006 CIA report included in the 1,600 documents reviewed by the NMAP? If it was, there is no evidence that this important piece of information, perhaps the one that mattered most for their mission to "focus on algebra," had any impact on its recommendations. There was an attempt to compare teaching activities and practices from other countries, but they missed the essential ingredients that would have enhanced the learning process for our students. The following is one of the key NMAP observations:

> *Studies of children in the United States, comparisons of these children with children from other nations with higher mathematics achievement, and even cross-generational changes within the United States indicate that many contemporary U.S. children do not reach the point of fast and efficient solving of single-digit addition, subtraction, multiplication, and division with whole numbers, much less fluent execution of more complex algorithms as early as children in many other countries. Surprisingly, many never gain such proficiency.*[41]

There was nothing new or groundbreaking in that statement. It was merely a statement of the facts as gleaned from the research. Observe that emphasis is given to the four basic operations (addition, multiplication, subtraction, and division) with "whole numbers." The fact is that the four basic operations on whole numbers continues to be beaten to death throughout the elementary school experience, and negative numbers have been ignored, and are introduced much too late in the American mathematics curriculum. Recall that the teacher input to NMAP was "More focus on positive vs. negative numbers." There is no mention of this necessary set of numbers that offers the number-sense that is the key to beginning algebra. We will get to the issue of numbers and number-sense, and the importance of mastering the four basic operations on all sets of numbers in chapters 3, 4, and 5.

Continuing inquiry led me to the metrication chart in figure 2.2. You'll observe that the United States, this behemoth of an industrialized country, is conspicuously absent from the list of countries currently using the metric system. This is confirmation of the 2006 CIA report.

The table in figure 2.2 shows that starting with France in 1795, and Austria and Germany in the 1870s, Russia and China in 1925, and Japan in 1957, the large industrialized countries—except Great Britain, the British Commonwealth countries, and the United States—went metric before 1960. The delay of Great Britain and the United States to adapt to metric is understandable from a historical and cultural perspective, since the latter originated as a colony of the former. Had President George Washington had his way, the United State would have been at the head of the list together with France, since his presidency was from 1789 to 1797.[42] But the chart shows that starting in the 1960s, Great Britain and most of the British Commonwealth countries such as Canada, Australia, South Africa, Kenya, Tanzania, Uganda and New Zealand also adopted the metric system as the official system of measurements. Jamaica, a British Commonwealth country and the last entry on the list in figure 2.2, sided with the United States until 1998, when it too opted to adopt the metric system. Isn't it truly ironic that in 1965 Great Britain and its commonwealth of nations abandoned the British system of measurements, yet that discarded and relatively archaic and outdated system from the country of origin is currently the prime utility for measurements in commerce and in the education of our children in the United States? It now goes under the name the "US Customary System" (USCS) of measurements.

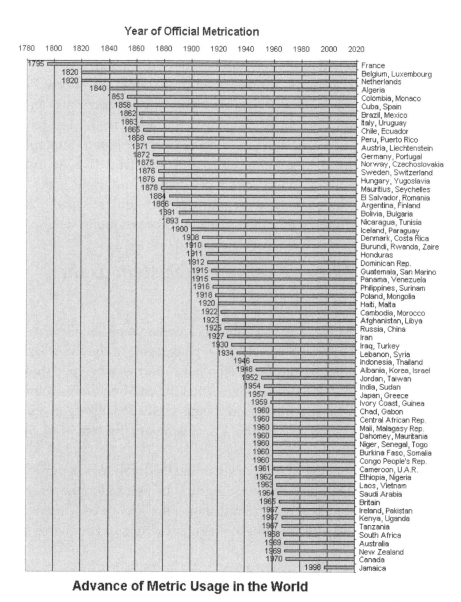

Figure 2.2: *Source: http://lamar.colostate.edu/~hillger/internat.htm*

The following stark fact is evident. When both charts, i.e., figure 2.1 and figure 2.2, are compared, the countries in which fifteen-year-old students outperformed the United States are all on the metric system, while the United States continues to use the USCS. If utilization of the metric system is a key educational resource for mathematics and science, figure 2.2 shows that the United Kingdom, (Great Britain), Australia, Canada, and New Zealand as well as the comparatively small country of Jamaica are all ahead of the United States.

These facts prompt at least two fundamental questions. First, if we spend more money per student than any other country in the world, why can't the United States place at least in the top ten on the PISA tests, as is the case with countries like Japan, Singapore, Finland, and the British Commonwealth countries like Australia, New Zealand, and Canada? Second, what, if anything, does the metric system have to do with mathematics and science? We'll answer the first question in section 2.2 and the second in section 2.3.

2.2 United States Customary System as the Culprit

There must be a cause-and-effect explanation as to why the United States is getting these very low placements in the PISA tests in spite of the fact that we outspend all other countries when per-student cost is measured. The evidence shows that the children of this country, before they get to age fifteen, are being educationally deprived by the continued utilization of the US Customary System (USCS) of measurements.

This cumbersome system, (see the first three columns in figure 2.3) measuring weights, capacity, and length, is being used in the teaching of mathematics, with serious ramifications for science education, and it is reinforced by utilization in the regular culture, in commerce, and in the economy

Figure 2.3 is only a partial list. You can see the full listing by looking at the indicated page of the Merriam-Webster website indicated as the source of this information. Please observe that there are eighteen measures in the USCS on this page alone, but each one has a metric equivalent.

WEIGHT AND MEASURES

UNITS	ABBREVIATION OR SYMBOL	EQUIVALENTS IN OTHER UNITS OF SAME SYSTEM	METRIC EQUIVALENT
WEIGHT			
short hundredweight		100 pounds, 0.05 short ton	45.359 kilograms
long hundredweight		112 pounds, 0.05 long ton	50.802 kilograms
pound	lb *or* lb avdp *also* #	16 ounces, 7000 grains	0.454 kilogram
ounce	oz *or* oz avdp	16 drams, 437.5 grains, 0.0625 pound	28.350 grams
dram	dr *or* dr avdp	27.344 grains, 0.0625 ounce	1.772 grams
grain	gr	0.037 dram, 0.002286 ounce	0.0648 gram
CAPACITY			
US liquid measure			
gallon	gal	4 quarts (231 cubic inches)	3.785 liters
quart	qt	2 pints (57.75 cubic inches)	0.946 liter
pint	pt	4 gills (28.875 cubic inches)	473.176 milliliters
gill	gi	4 fluid ounces (7.219 cubic inches)	118.294 milliliters
fluid ounce	fl oz	8 fluid drams (1.805 cubic inches)	29.573 milliliters
fluid drams	fl dr	60 minims (0.226 cubic inch)	3.697 milliliters
minim	min	1/60 fluid dram (0.003760 cubic inch)	0.061610 milliliter
LENGTH			
mile	mi	5280 feet, 1760 yards, 320 rods	1.609 kilometers
rod	rd	5.5 yards, 16.5 feet	5.029 meters
yard	yd	3 feet, 36 inches	0.9144 meter
foot	ft *or* '	12 inches, 0.333 yard	30.48 centimeters
inch	in *or* "	0.083 foot, 0.028 yard	2.54 centimeters

Figure 2.3: *Source: http://www2.merriam-webster.com/mw/table/weight.htm*

In the fourth column, all eighteen distinct USCS measures are expressed, as multiples or submultiples, in only one of three metric measures, i.e., the **meter**, the **gram**, or the **liter**. I will later show that reduction of the number of measures on this page, from eighteen down to three, would be like removing clutter from the children's mathematics and science curriculum, thus providing an ordered, clear, synchronous, symmetric, and seamless path to the core concepts of mathematics and science. Consider two simple examples used for length or distance. Wouldn't it be much easier for a child learn that one kilometer is 1000 meters than to remember that one mile is 5280 feet? How about the meter being 100 centimeters versus one yard being 36 inches? And yet the meter and its associated constituents, consisting of multiples or decimalized parts (submultiples), contain the units used in science classes for scientific measurements from the micro to the macro levels of length.

We mentioned before that Great Britain abandoned the British system of measurements and converted to metric. The British pre-metric currency had at least eleven parts: namely, the guinea, the pound, the crown, the half crown, the florin, the shilling, the sixpence, the three pence, the penny, the half penny, and the farthing. I was educated in that currency system, called "pounds, shillings, and pence." This was the currency system that George Washington abandoned and replaced it with the US dollar. In that archaic British currency system, the calculations for simple addition and subtraction were both unnecessarily difficult and time-consuming for the middle- and lower-performing students. British metrication has swept away all that clutter of eleven currency parts and replaced it with only one. It is called the **pound sterling**. The pound is decimalized, with one sub-multiple, where one pound is equal to 100 pennies, just like the US dollar, where one dollar is 100 cents. When the US won its independence from Great Britain, one of its most significant initiatives was the creation of a decimalized currency that is the American dollar. With this change to the immensely simpler currency, the US has always been way ahead of Great Britain. Adding and subtracting dollars and cents is so easy that it is used as an effective mnemonic to teach addition and subtraction of decimals in US schools. It will be shown in chapter 6 that if the

United States were to replace the eighteen USCS measures found in figure 2.3 with the three utilitarian metric measures for length, weight, and capacity, respectively called the **meter**, the **gram**, and the **liter**, it would be like the British reduction of eleven currency units to only one, thus creating more ease of use and facilitating mathematics education. The ease of use of the pattern-based metric system and the savings in mental energy and time required for memorization of the cluttered USCS measurements system would provide the fundamental basis for reform of our mathematics and science education curriculum, with modifications focusing on the lower grades.

There is no value-added necessity to continue with the USCS's cluttered list of measures, some of which are hardly ever used in practice. There is no cognitive advantage for children to learn, for example, that a mile is 5280 feet. It is a virtual nightmare for the middle- and lower-performing American student to have to add or subtract measurements involving short hundredweight or short tons, long hundredweight or long tons, pounds, ounces, drams, and grains. In a metric educational environment, these measures are reduced to multiples or submultiples of the **gram**. The same is true for problems involving units of capacity such as gallons, quarts, pints, gills, fluid ounce, fluid dram, and minim, which can be similarly reduced to multiples or submultiples of the **liter**. In like manner, problems involving miles, furlong, rods, yards, feet, and inches can be reduced to multiples or submultiples of the **meter**.

Perpetuation of this educational clutter will be a guarantee that fifteen-year-old students of the United States will continue to be at a devastating disadvantage. Not only that, if nothing is done, US students will continue to have less than mediocre performances on international tests, making the financial resources being expended on misguided and untested programs a wasteful squandering of taxpayers' money.

One of the serious longer-range consequences for this country is that it will have to continue to recruit scientists and engineers from metric system countries in order to fill related job vacancies here at home. Even more ominous is the threat that large industrial countries such as China, Russia, Germany, and Japan will ultimately surpass the United States in world supremacy, particularly in engineering technology.

The British newspaper *The Daily Mail* reported that China and Russia have mutual plans to build a high-speed railway connecting Moscow and Beijing.[43] Recent reports state that the project has been actualized. Of even greater significance is that the *Washington Post* has stated that China is considering building a similar high-speed train to the West Coast of the United States via Alaska.[44] If these projects are carried out, we can be sure they will be in metric units. This was the case with completion of the undersea megaproject called the "Chunnel," which currently links Great Britain and France under the twenty-one-mile-wide English Channel. Compare these constructions with the fact that the United States doesn't even have a high-speed train from our East Coast to the West Coast. If we were to build one, it would be in USCS units, a boost for US commerce, but unfortunately a loss of opportunity for US education. I could see a scenario where we might have to hire Chinese, Russian, French, or British engineers who were involved in the construction of the Chunnel to build our own high-speed rail system—if we ever build one of such magnitude.

2.3 The Importance of the Metric System for Mathematics and Science

Now we get to the second fundamental question. What does the metric system have to do with science and mathematics education?

The three writers Gordon Uno, Richard Story, and Randy More have described the metric system as it relates to the United States as follows:

> The **metric system** is a standardized system of measurement used by scientists throughout the world. It is also the measurement system used in everyday life in most countries. Although the metric system is the only measurement system ever acknowledged by Congress, the United States remains "out of step" with the rest of the world by clinging to the antiquated English system of measurements involving pounds, inches, and so on.

Metric units commonly used in biology include:
meter *(m) The basic unit of length*
liter *(L) The basic unit of volume*
gram *(g) The basic unit of mass*
degree Celsius *(°C) The basic unit of temperature.*

Source: *http://www.mhhe.com/biosci/pae/botany/uno/student/olc/ metric.mhtml.*

Please take note of the part of the statement by writers Uno, Storey, and More that even though "the metric system is the only measurement system ever acknowledged by Congress, the United States remains 'out of step' with the rest of the world." More will be said about this later.

The four categories of the metric system i.e., the three units of length, volume, and mass, together with the measure for temperature, are attributes that simultaneously attest to its simplicity and to its power as a tool for both mathematics and science.

In chapter 5, there will be graphic illustration showing how the Celsius Scale matches perfectly with the real number system, the indispensible tool used in mathematics education starting in kindergarten, and how it can accelerate the learning of basic algebraic concepts much earlier than is the current practice in the US. In chapter 6, we will explore the intricacies of the pure metric system (units of mass, length, and volume), again with graphic illustration as to how it is perfect for mathematics, beginning in the early grades of our K–12 system of education. The real advantage of the metric system will be made clear, not only in its ease of use, but its symmetric characteristics with the numbers we use in daily lives as well as in science. It will become clear why we must abandon the USCS, which hangs over US mathematics and science education like the sword of Damocles.

2.4 The United States Approach to Metrication

You may recall that in the introduction I indicated that the pure metric system, unlike the Celsius Scale, has a history of use in the United States. Indeed, there is a history, but it is one that is replete with indecisive congressional action to fully commit to a complete national replacement of the USCS with the metric system. This lack of complete national conversion has resulted in at least one very costly incident in the space program, about which more will be said later.

Even though George Washington was unsuccessful in changing to metric in his time during the late 1700s, in 1875 the United States recognized that the metric system was more in line with international measurement systems and was one of seventeen signatory nations to the Treaty of the Meter.[45] In 1893 it was proposed that metric units be adopted as the "fundamental standards for length and mass."[46] Decades later in 1965, the United Kingdom, the originator of the imperial system of measures, began transitioning to the metric system to align itself with the measures of the European Common Market.[47] In 1968, by an act of the US Congress, a three-year study was authorized to determine the feasibility of adopting the metric system. The final report of that study, entitled *A Metric America: A Decision Whose Time Has Come*,[48] concluded that conversion to the metric system was "in the best interest of the nation because of foreign trade and the increasing influence of technology in American life."[49] The study recommended that the United States implement a "carefully planned transition to the predominant use of the metric system over a ten-year period." The Congress then passed the "Metric Conversion Act of1975,"[50] but left out the "carefully planned transition over ten years" conversion requirement. (Much more will be said about this in chapter 7.) The US Metric Board (USMB) was established, but the lack of a congressional mandate to carry out a comprehensive national conversion resulted in a process of voluntary conversations. The ineffectiveness of the USMB resulted in its disestablishment in 1982.[51] The continued need for alignment with international standards to facilitate trade, motivated Congress to revisit the issue in 1988. They passed legislation to amend or replace the "Metric Conversion Act of 1975" with the "Omnibus Trade and Competitiveness Act of 1988."[52] But this new legislation served merely as a prompt to adopt the metric system for weights and measures for trade and commerce and was tentative at best. The Fahrenheit scale for temperatures would remain in place. The new legislation stated that government has an obligation to assist the private sector, but only where there is voluntary compliance.[53] The process of voluntary compliance and lack of mandate without a timeline for a comprehensive program of national conversion had serious consequences not only for science and mathematics education but also for the space program.

In 1995, NASA had to absorb a loss of $125 million when its Mars Climate Orbiter malfunctioned as it maneuvered to orbit the planet Mars. The result was a fiery destruction of the spacecraft. Inquiry into the cause of failure found that the two principal agencies involved in the design of the spacecraft used different measurement systems. One used metric, while the other used USCS units. The mismatch resulted in lack of systems coordination at a critical moment when the spacecraft entered the Martian atmosphere.[54] In light of the fact that, as mentioned earlier, Gordon Uno et al. pointed out that "the metric system is the only measurement system ever acknowledged by Congress," this incident should never have happened. It's another occasion where the indecisiveness and arbitrariness of the Congress resulted in an indifferent, casual, and unnecessary waste of taxpayers' money.

In the next chapter, we'll explore the principal parts of the real number system and how it is partitioned at different grade levels. This is a necessary precursor to making the case that the Celsius scale, rather than the Fahrenheit scale, is a perfect instrument for early acquaintance with negative numbers and algebraic concepts. We will also revisit some of the fundamental concepts in elementary school mathematics. This is in preparation for demonstrating the deleterious effect of the absence of negative numbers in the mathematics curriculum before the sixth grade. We will later explore how these numbers could be introduced in very early grades, much earlier than is the current practice, if we lived in a Celsius environment.

Chapter 3:
The Real Number System as the Basis for Algebra

As a framework for demonstrating the efficacy of the Celsius scale for mathematics education, we will take a layman's look at the real number system on which K–12 mathematics is based. We will then look at the traditional focus on pure arithmetic,[55] which comprises the mathematics curriculum at the elementary school level. We will go on to look at how the Celsius scale would provide the early nurturing environment with negative numbers, which are normally excluded in K–5 mathematics. It is these numbers that would provide the number sense that is necessary for optimal proficiency in K–12 mathematics in general and in algebra in particular. This will prepare us for the core of this letter, which will be presented in chapters 5, 6, and 7. We will then be able to have an understanding as to why a metric system country like Russia can start algebra early in elementary school,[56] while we in the United State, limited by the USCS system, start this important area of mathematics as late as the ninth grade.

3.1 The Real Number System and the Number Line

The number line in figure 3.1 represents all the "real numbers" upon which the algebraic system in mathematics is constructed. Some of the details in this section maybe a little abstract or technical for some readers. Even if you read in a cursory manner, I suggest that you absorb what you can, or even skip it, but please make sure you keep in mind a visual picture of the "number line" and its constituent parts as shown in figure 3.1, because it plays a very important conceptual role in elementary school mathematics. I will be returning to it later in chapters 5, 6, and 10.

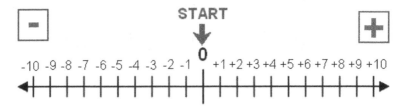

Figure 3.1: *Source: http://www.green-planet-solar-energy.com/ support-files/number-line*

The real number line is a geometric utility in mathematics and is a graphic representation of the real number system. It provides a conceptual basis for arithmetic, algebra, geometry, trigonometry, coordinate geometry, calculus, and more.

The real number system consists of six categories of numbers, with each category requiring mastery of the four basic operations (addition, subtraction, multiplication, and division) before they can be effectively applied to the areas of mathematics previously stated, and then used to facilitate problem solving. Using set notation,[57] each sub category or subset of the real numbers can be represented by the first five sets below. Please bear with me on 4, 5, and 6 for now. They are included for mathematical completeness to "fill out" the number line. These are some of the abstractions you may skip, since they are not fundamental to understand the thrust of this letter. I will attempt to explain them later in layman's language:

1. The natural or counting numbers: {1,2,3,4,…}
2. The whole numbers: {0,1,2,3,4,…}
3. The integers: {…−3,−2,−1, 0, +1, +2, +3,…}
4. The rational numbers (fractions): { $\frac{a}{b}$ | a and b are integers, and b≠0}. Rational numbers, commonly referred to as fractions, can be written as terminating decimal or non-terminating repeating decimals. For example, $\frac{2}{5}$ can be written as 0.4, and $\frac{2}{3}$ can be written as the repeating decimal 0.666… and represented symbolically as $0.\overline{6}$
5. The irrational numbers: written in set form as { x | x is a non-terminating, non-repeating decimal}. In other words, irrational numbers cannot be written as fractions. Two such numbers are π (π = 3.14159…) and √2 (√2 = 1.4142…).
6. The real number system: { x | x can be written as a decimal}. This simply means that every number on the number line can be written as a decimal. For example, the number zero can be written as 0 or 0.000… The number 4 can be written as 4.0 or 4.0000… Four dollars can be written as $4 or $4.00. This real number system is the totality or the union of all the preceding five sets.[58]

Every point on the number line is associated with a number. In geometry, a point is considered to have no dimensions (no length, no width, and no height). This makes the number line a continuous geometric construct (with no gaps) of points extending in opposite directions. The arrows at the ends of the number line indicate that the numbers continue ad infinitum in both directions. The line is divided into equal demarcations by the integers. Thus, these numbers can be listed as discrete and ordered elements of the set of **counting numbers**, the set of **whole numbers**, and the set of **integers**. Note that the whole numbers contain all the counting numbers, and the integers contain all the whole numbers and the counting numbers. In other words, a counting number is an integer, and a whole number is also an integer. All other real numbers are on the line between the integers. These other numbers, although ordered, cannot be listed discretely, because they are points continuously attached to each other to form the number line.

We know, for example, that the whole number 9 is followed in order by the whole number 10. But it is impossible to state the next fraction in order after the fraction $\frac{2}{5}$. Knowledge of the constituent sets of numbers on the number line is essential for the study of mathematics at all levels from elementary school through college and university.

3.2 The Real Number Line for Algebra and Beyond

The great mathematician and philosopher Rene Descartes used the real number line to create coordinate geometry.[59] Figure 3.2, shows how two number lines are perpendicularly positioned to create a plane, which is referred to as the Cartesian plane, a name that gives credit to its creator, but the most commonly used name in mathematics classes or textbooks is the rectangular coordinate plane. The rectangular coordinate plane takes us from one-dimensional space, i.e., the number line, to two dimensions, i.e., the plane. You'll observe that the two number lines divide the plane into four numbered parts called quadrants. Using the abbreviation Q for quadrants, these four parts are numbered counterclockwise as QI, QII, QIII, and QIV. This creates a reference grid for locating points in the plane represented by numbers called coordinates. Each coordinate point is identified by two numbers, conventionally labeled in variable form as (x,y). The number represented by x (the x coordinate) is taken from the horizontal number line called the x-axis, and the number represented by y (the y coordinate) is taken from the vertical number line called the y-axis. You'll observe that with the point (−3,2) represented by the black dot in QII, the number −3 is read from the x-axis and the number 2 is read from the y-axis. This rectangular coordinate structure is essential for a course in algebra. In fact, this takes students from the world of discrete mathematics and introduces them to continuous mathematics, setting them on a direct path to the study of calculus. If you randomly flip through the pages of a calculus textbook, you'll see the rectangular coordinate chart as a ubiquitous graphic throughout the text.

As you look at the signs of the numbers in each quadrant, I implore you to recall the idée fixe of this letter, that mathematics teachers suggested to the NMAP that there should be "More focus on positive vs. negative numbers."

Using the elements of the rectangular coordinate system, Sir Isaac Newton in Great Britain and Gottfried Leibnitz in Germany used coordinate geometry to create calculus.[60] Mathematics, with its applications in the sciences, has not been the same since then, and most of the technological and engineering advances we take for granted today, such as the remote we use for television, the cell phone, the light bulb, the complete mapping of the human genome, would be impossible without calculus.

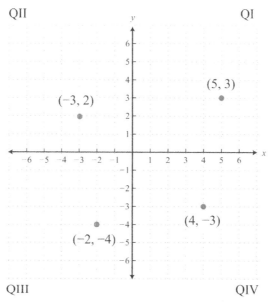

Figure 3.2: *Source: http://2012books.lardbucket.org/books/beginning-algebra/s06-01-rectangular-coordinate-system.html*

In figure 3.3, quadrant I (QI) is being used for one of the important concepts in calculus called differentiation. Calculus is divided into two basic areas of study. One is called differential calculus, and the other is called integral calculus, and both areas utilize all four quadrants in the rectangular coordinate plane. There are many more exciting areas of exploration and applications for which calculus is the basic platform.

For example, after completing calculus, students go on to study differential equations, which provide scientists and engineers with an indispensable set of mathematical concepts for practical applications, and the study of what are referred to as wave functions. I'm tempted to go to more exciting areas of study, but let's not get away from our inquiry.

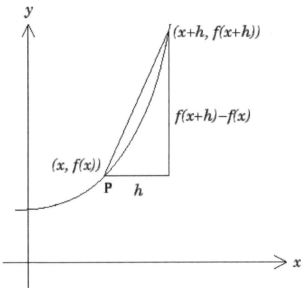

Figure 3.3: *Source: http://www.eldamar.org.uk/maths/calculus/node2. html*

If you were able to understand everything said above, kudos to you. You have the potential to be a mathematician or a scientist or both. On the other hand, if you are not well grounded in mathematics, some of this may seem somewhat abstract. You are not lost if, as suggested, you focused on the number line and the importance of teacher input to the NMAP that "More focus on positive vs. negative numbers" is essential for American students to start algebra in the early grades.

We will now take a look at the constituent parts of elementary school mathematics as it is taught in this country. This is necessary to make the case that implementation of the metric system with the Celsius scale would be a fundamental game changer for the how mathematics is taught at this level.

3.3 Inadequacy of Arithmetic in Elementary Schools

In most elementary schools across the United States, starting in kindergarten, the core of the mathematics curriculum is based on arithmetic. Primary emphasis is given to mastery of the four basic operations: addition, subtraction, multiplication, and division of positive numbers. These include whole numbers, fractions, and decimals.

The positive numbers, starting with zero, are restricted to the right side of the number line, as seen in figure 3.1. The positive integers, {+1, +2, +3, +4...}, all have a positive (plus) sign attached, as seen on the number line; but in arithmetic they are written without signs and are called counting or natural numbers as represented by the set {1,2,3,4...}. This conventional practice removes the ambiguity of confusing the positive sign "+", which distinguishes that a number is on the right side of the number line, with the plus sign "+," which is used for the operation of addition. Thus, in elementary school, if we wanted to add the two positive numbers +4 and +6 we would simply write that addition problem as 4 + 6 to get an answer of 10, rather than (+4) + (+6) to get an answer of +10. The number zero has no sign. By including zero with the counting numbers, we have the set of whole numbers {0,1,2,3...}.[61] Beginning in first grade, American students are taught to master the four basic operations on whole numbers.

+	0	1	2	3	4	5	6	7	8	9	10
0	0	1	2	3	4	5	6	7	8	9	10
1	1	2	3	4	5	6	7	8	9	10	11
2	2	3	4	5	6	7	8	9	10	11	12
3	3	4	5	6	7	8	9	10	11	12	13
4	4	5	6	7	8	9	10	11	12	13	14
5	5	6	7	8	9	10	11	12	13	14	15
6	6	7	8	9	10	11	12	13	14	15	16
7	7	8	9	10	11	12	13	14	15	16	17
8	8	9	10	11	12	13	14	15	16	17	18
9	9	10	11	12	13	14	15	16	17	18	19
10	10	11	12	13	14	15	16	17	18	19	20

Figure 3.4: *Addition Table Chart*

An elementary school teacher will suggest that your youngster must master elementary "addition facts" (see figure 3.4) and basic "multiplication facts" (see figure 3.5). I will have some suggestion, in the postscripts of this letter, as to how parents can help their youngsters master the facts in each table as quickly as possible.

×	1	2	3	4	5	6	7	8	9	10
1	1	2	3	4	5	6	7	8	9	10
2	2	4	6	8	10	12	14	16	18	20
3	3	6	9	12	15	18	21	24	27	30
4	4	8	12	16	20	24	28	32	36	40
5	5	10	15	20	25	30	35	40	45	50
6	6	12	18	24	30	36	42	48	54	60
7	7	14	21	28	35	42	49	56	63	70
8	8	16	24	32	40	48	56	64	72	80
9	9	18	27	36	45	54	63	72	81	90
10	10	20	30	40	50	60	70	80	90	100

Figure 3.5: *Multiplication Table Chart*

3.4 Rational Numbers in Elementary School

Rational numbers, otherwise called fractions, include the whole numbers and some of the numbers between them on the number line.[62] A rational number is formed using two integers separated by a horizontal line called a fraction bar. For example, the fraction $\frac{2}{5}$ is a rational number. The integer above the fraction bar is called the numerator, and the integer below is called the denominator. The denominator tells us the number of equal parts into which an object called the "whole" is divided. The numerator tells us how many parts of the whole we have selected at a particular moment. This very important concept is elaborated on in figure 3.6, which shows a graphic representation of the fraction $\frac{1}{4}$.

Any integer can be used for the numerator, and any integer, except for zero,[63] can be used in the denominator. (More will be said later about why division by zero is not allowed in mathematics.) This means that any integer can be expressed as a fraction, by making that integer the numerator and 1 the denominator. For example, the integer 7 can be written as the fraction $\frac{7}{1}$ without loss of value. Unlike integers, which, as stated before, can be listed consecutively, there are no such things as consecutive fractions in mathematics, unless defined by a particular sequence of fractions.

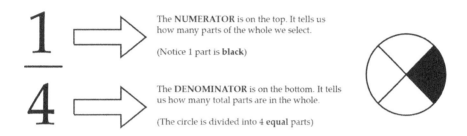

The **NUMERATOR** is on the top. It tells us how many parts of the whole we select.

(Notice 1 part is **black**)

The **DENOMINATOR** is on the bottom. It tells us how many total parts are in the whole.

(The circle is divided into 4 **equal** parts)

Figure 3.6

Depending on the rational number (or fraction), it can be written as a terminating or repeating decimal. For example, $\frac{5}{8} = 0.625$, and $\frac{1}{3} = 0.3333\ldots$ As a shortcut, a repeating decimal can be written with a bar over the repeating decimal digit or digits. For example, $\frac{1}{3} = 0.\overline{3}$ and since the fraction $\frac{2}{11} = 0.18181818\ldots$, we can write this as $0.\overline{18}$. Decimals are special fractions with denominators of 10, 100, 1000, and so on. For example, $0.8 = \frac{8}{10}$, $0.47 = \frac{47}{100}$, $0.031 = \frac{31}{1000}$, and so on. As for percents, the word "percent," which uses the symbol "%," is interpreted to mean "over 100." Hence percent expressions are shortcuts for fractions that have 100 as the denominator. For example, $50\% = \frac{50}{100}$. If necessary, percent can be used to represent a whole number. For example, $400\% = \frac{400}{100} = \frac{4}{1} = 4$. This means that if you invested $1000 in the stock market, and your investment grew 400%, you would have made $4000 on top of the $1000 you originally invested. You would now have $1000 + $4000 = $5000.

A denominator of a fraction is also a divisor. The fraction $\frac{5}{8}$ listed above is the same as 5 divided by 8. If you use your calculator to do the division $5 \div 8$ you'll get the equivalent decimal, 0.625. We mentioned earlier that the whole number 7 can be written as the fraction $\frac{7}{1}$. Note that when 7 is divided by 1, the answer is 7. Because of the division principle, the number 1 can be written as a fraction in an infinite number of ways, such as $\frac{1}{1}, \frac{2}{2}, \frac{3}{3}, \frac{4}{4}$, and so on. If we use a symbol, such as the letter x, to represent any non-zero number, we would be correct if we wrote that $\frac{x}{x}$ has the same numerical value as the number 1. The general proposition is that any number except zero divided by itself is equal to 1.

Unfortunately, because of American elementary schools' focus on mastery of arithmetic operations on whole numbers and fractions, the numbers to the left of zero on the number line, i.e., the negative numbers, are customarily excluded below grade 6 in the United States. I will later illustrate that in countries with the metric system and the Celsius scale, negative numbers such as −2, −5, and −10 are a part of daily life of prekindergarten and elementary school children during the winter months. In fact, if our elementary school children lived in a Celsius environment, where during the winter months negative numbers shape behavioral activities, we could easily extend representations of the number 1 to the left side of the number line, to include fractional forms such as ..., $\frac{-4}{-4}, \frac{-3}{-3}, \frac{-2}{-2}, \frac{-1}{-1}$. An expression such as $\frac{-4}{-4} = 1$ would embed in the elementary school student's mind that a negative number divided by a negative number gives a positive answer. This is a key concept for beginning algebra, and it can start long before the fifth grade.

3.5 Irrational Numbers in Elementary Schools

In the interest of completeness with respect to the number line, we'll now discuss irrational numbers. The existence of rational numbers, which can be written as fractions, implicitly suggests the existence of irrational numbers, which cannot be written as fractions, because they are non-terminating, non-repeating decimals. Indeed, there are such numbers, but they are not generally studied in elementary school. One exception is the number pi, which is positioned between the whole numbers 3 and 4 on the number line. It is conventionally represented by the Greek letter π, where π = 3.14159..., which in itself is a non-terminating, non-repeating decimal. Pi is one of the most interesting numbers in the history of mathematics. It dates back to the ancient Egyptian and Babylonian civilizations, and it is determined by the ratio (a comparison of two measures) of the circumference (C) of a circle to its diameter (D).[64] This relation, see figure 3.7, is written as the formula $\pi = \frac{C}{D}$, meaning that π is obtained by dividing the circumference (C) by the diameter (D).

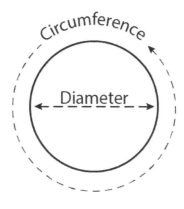

Figure 3.7

Because of the non-terminating nature of π, no human being is capable of calculating the exact numerical value of the circumference of a circle. For practical purposes, even for engineers and scientists, the number π has to be approximated for use. In elementary through high school classes, the approximation takes the value as 3.14 or the fraction $\frac{22}{7}$. In science classes where precise measures are needed, the approximation may extend the decimal to 3.14159. In ancient times, the Egyptians used an approximation of 3, which is pi rounded off to the nearest whole number. With this value, the circumference of a circle is calculated as 3 times the diameter, which is a pretty good approximation, depending on the level of accuracy that is needed in a particular project. If you take any circular figure such as your wedding ring or a hula-hoop and measure the diameter, you can get a close approximation of the circumference of each by simply multiplying the length of the diameter by 3. Obviously, using the 3 as the approximation of pi will give a circumference that is a smidgen shorter than the actual circumference.

You as a parent, or your children, would have lots of fun reading the book *The Joy of π*, by David Blatner. There, you will learn more about the evolution and intrigues of pi. One interesting fact in particular is that the decimal digit in the millionth place is the number 1. There is also a number in the billionth place and one in the trillionth place,[65] and so on, because of the non-terminating nature of pi.

One of the best graphics of the non-terminating nature of this special number is seen in figure 3.8.

Each year, most schools in the country celebrate "Pi Day," on March 14 or 3/14, (a play upon the 3.14 value of pi). As indicated in figure 3.8, that date is also Albert Einstein's birthday. The year 2015 had special interest because the date 3/14/15 is also the first five digits (3.1415) of pi. You may want to call your school as the date 3/14 approaches each year and seek to attend or participate in the celebration. Some schools do a food play on phonetics, and so you may even be served a scrumptious slice of your favorite **pie**.

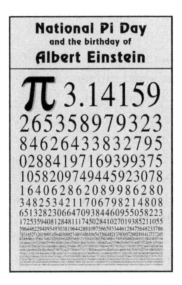

Figure 3.8

CHAPTER 4:
K–12 Mathematics Curricula and Negative Numbers

We have taken a cursory look at US elementary school mathematics and have seen that it is restricted to positive numbers. These are all the numbers to the right of zero on the number line, toward positive infinity. The progression to infinity satisfies one of the axioms of mathematics that "There is no largest number." This means that no matter how large a number we can state or name, we can always add 1 to it to get a greater number.

We will now take a broader but cursory look at the K–12 curriculum as it relates to negative numbers, which as we recall are on the left of zero progressing toward negative infinity on the number line.

A sample of state mathematics curricula around the country before the Common Core State Standards (CCSS) were implemented shows that negative numbers are introduced, with few exceptions, in the sixth grade. At this level, students encounter negative numbers for the first time and are merely taught to locate them on the number line. Introduction of the four basic operations on the integers, which include negative and positive numbers, is delayed for later grades. It will be shown later that countries like Russia, a metric system country with a Celsius environment, actually start these operations as early as the first grade.

In some school systems in our country, these operations are not introduced before the seventh grade for the better-than-average student, and as late as the ninth grade for others. I worked as a mathematics teacher from 1970 through 1995 in New York City. Over this period, I taught in the inner-city high schools Prospect Heights in Brooklyn and Evander Childs in the Bronx, and served as assistant principal— supervision of mathematics[66] at W. H. Taft, also in the Bronx. In these and most high schools in New York City, the integers and other signed numbers along with the four basic operations were taught as introductory concepts in the ninth grade in beginning algebra. It is important to note that in grade 9, most students are at or approaching age fifteen, the age for taking the PISA test.

Difficulties occur mostly with operating on binary combinations of signed numbers (negative and/or positive numbers), because, unlike students in a Celsius culture, the set of negative numbers is not a regular utility in the daily lives of American students. For example, the addition problem (+2) + (−5) is an application of the binary operation of addition (+) on the two integers +2 and −5, with each number taken from different sides of the number line. Using the "rules" for addition of signed numbers, the answer is −3. Problems of this type can be found in ninth-grade textbooks in beginning algebra across the US. Here again it will be shown later in chapter 5 how elementary school students in Celsius cultures such as Canada, Finland, the United Kingdom, Russia, Australia, and France can easily get the correct answer. They do so not by knowing the "rules" of addition of signed numbers, but by intuition from experiential knowledge. This is accomplished through utilitarian experience with the Celsius scale. In addition, a Celsius thermometer or enlarged Celsius chart, when placed on the classroom wall (see figure 5.1 and figure 5.2 in chapter 5) is actually a vertical segment of the number line with both negative and positive numbers.

At the community college level, many adult students who must repeat K–12 mathematics, beginning at the developmental level, experience difficulties with performing binary operations on combinations of negative and positive numbers. In my most recent job as a mathematics professor at Passaic County Community College in New Jersey, I encountered adult students who struggled with these concepts, even though they were very capable with regular arithmetic with positive numbers. Adult students in metric system countries have no such problems, because of their early orientation even as preschoolers to negative numbers on the Celsius scale.

As any mathematics teacher will tell you, mastery in the ability to perform the four basic operations on all real numbers, i.e., negative and positive numbers, is absolutely essential for success in algebra.

The following is a statement by Sarah Hagan, a high school mathematics teacher in the state of Oklahoma, on a web site called "Math Equals Love."

> *The ability to successfully add/subtract/multiply/divide*
> *integers is going to be crucial for their future success at*
> *solving equations and graphing. If my students do not*
> *master these basics, they will not be able to solve equations,*
> *even if they understand the concept of solving an equation.*[67]

To demonstrate what Sarah Hagan is saying, let's take a look at an assignment involving two equations.
Find a value for the letter x that would make each mathematical sentence (equation) true.

1. $5 + x = 8$

2. $6 + x = 2$

An elementary school student ensconced in a whole number environment could easily solve the first equation, since the whole number 3 makes the statement true. In the second equation, however, an elementary school student who is unaware of negative numbers would have difficulty finding the answer to make the statement true, because there is no whole number that can be added to 6 to get an answer of 2.

In a Celsius environment, an elementary school student could easily deduce that the only number that would make the statement true is −4. Solution is possible and easy only if the students are familiar with negative numbers.

The absence of negative numbers as a real life utility and the necessity of acquiring the ability to perform the four operations on positive and negative numbers was completely missed by the NMAP initiative. As previously stated, at best the idea of negative numbers was overlooked or at worst it was ignored. This was the critical nature of the input from mathematics teachers that there should be "More focus on positive vs. negative numbers."

In beginning algebra, students must be able to apply the four basic operations with fluency to polynomial expressions. Polynomials are algebraic expressions containing positive or negative numbers as numerical coefficients. Since the coefficients are signed numbers, students who master the aforementioned skills will be armed with the necessary prerequisites to fluently perform polynomial operations.

Let's consider some simple examples of addition of polynomials, which can easily be done in elementary grades. Let's use the letter p to represent pears. Surely, if a student can add 6 + 4 from the right side of the number line to get 10, then they should be able to add 6p + 4p to get 10p, just as if they were adding 6 pears plus 4 pears to get 10 pears. This is an example of adding the monomial 6p to the monomial 4p. This is an easy and appropriate way to introduce algebra to elementary school students. When operations with negative numbers (from the left side of the number line) are involved, it will be easy to add (−6p) + (−4p) to get −10p.

The game of golf is one game that uses both negative and positive numbers. Young children who learn the game or watch it on TV in the US know that if a golfer made three birdies that's a score of −3. If the same golfer makes 4 more birdies (−4), the cumulative score is (−3) + (−4) = −7. This is an example of adding two numbers from the left side of the number line.

The inability to perform the four operations with signed numbers and with symbols will have consequences, not only with polynomials in themselves, but as demonstrated above, also when students are required to solve equations containing negative numbers. Countries that are on the metric system are able to introduce algebraic concepts from the first grade. I previously mentioned that in Russian schools, algebra starts at the elementary school level. In an article entitled "What Do We Know about the Teaching and Learning of Algebra in the Elementary Grades?," published by the National Council of Teachers of Mathematics (NCTM), it was stated that, "The Russian-based approach...emphasizes the teaching of algebra with symbols right from the first grade."[68]

It was mentioned in the Introduction that it was Russia that shocked the United States with the launch of the Sputnik satellite. You may be surprised to learn that the Russian practice of introducing algebra in elementary or even at the kindergarten level is available at selected schools right here in the United States. Here is a statement from the website for the "Russian School of Mathematics" (RSM):

> *The Russian School of Mathematics introduces its students to algebraic elements starting in kindergarten. By second grade, our students are already solving simple algebraic equations and understand the notion of functions. We believe **logic and critical thinking** skills can be developed at an early age and that algebra is an ideal tool for this cultivation. Our practices are rooted in the theories of Russian psychologist Lev Vygotsky and are supported by a growing body of research that has come to recognize what we have believed all along: young children's minds can benefit greatly from an early introduction to algebra.*[69]

In section 3.4, I made the statement, "If we use a symbol such as x to represent any non-zero number, we would be correct if we wrote that $\frac{x}{x}$ has the same numerical value as the number 1." It is prudent to add that, with two exceptions, any letter of the alphabet can be used to represent numbers. The two exceptions are the letters "o" and "i" because the first can be confused with the number 0 and the second can be confused with the number 1. In K–12 mathematics, beyond the ninth grade in the US, letters of the Greek alphabet (see the lowercase of all twenty-four letters in figure 4.1) are also utilized both in mathematics and in science. The first three letters, alpha (α), beta (β), and gamma (γ), are used in atomic physics to represent three different kinds of radiation. Take note of the sixteenth letter, pi (π), which was discussed in section 3.4. The upper case of π is Π, and it is used as a symbol to express the operation of multiplication of mathematical sequences. The eighth letter, theta (θ), is used to represent variable angles in trigonometry. The uppercase of the eighteenth letter, sigma (σ) is Σ, and it is used as a symbol to express sums of mathematical sequences, which are simply referred to as summations. This symbol, Σ, will appear again in Postscript #9 of this letter. Other letters of the Greek alphabet are used throughout mathematics and the sciences.

Figure 4.1

While most of the Greek letter symbols will not be encountered until the later grades in K–12 mathematics, students with a firm grasp of algebraic concepts in the very early grades can then move on to mastery of simple equations, systems of equations, quadratic equations, and on to applications long before grade 9 or age fifteen. Early mastery will allow them to move on, with confidence, to the more exciting levels of mathematics such as intermediate algebra, the even more exciting study of trigonometry, and on to the exhilarating study of the utilitarian continuous mathematics in calculus, all before completing high school.

In this country, calculus (differential and integral) and its applications are currently offered to selected students as an advanced placement course in high school for college credit. Other students take it in their first year of most colleges or universities in the United States.

If we restructure our mathematics curriculum to simulate and enhance the Canadian or the Russian school models, there is no reason why both differential and integral calculus cannot be completed by the average American high school student, thus providing the precollege readiness skills needed for excelling in university-level mathematics and science. We can determine the efficacy of these suggestions by piloting, but Canada has done exactly what I'm suggesting. The following preparation for science and engineering students is taken from the Canadian mathematics curriculum for the 12th grade:

> *The Grade 12 university preparation course* **Calculus and Vectors** *is designed to prepare students for university programs, such as science, engineering, and economics... Calculus is introduced in the Rate of Change strand by extending the numeric and graphical representation of rates of change introduced in the Advanced Functions course to include more abstract algebraic representations. The Derivatives and Their Applications strand provides students with the opportunity to develop the algebraic and problem-solving skills needed to solve problems associated with rates of change. Prior knowledge of geometry and trigonometry is used in the Geometry and Algebra of Vectors strand to develop vector concepts that can be used to solve interesting problems, including those arising from real-world applications.*[70]

At a minimum, this is what is needed for an effective K–12 mathematics education across our country. It is to be understood that not every student may want to study engineering and science, but for those students who have that potential, the Canadian curriculum is structurally and comprehensively accommodating. It is age appropriate and designed to discover the talented mathematics students very early, and steps can be taken to nurture such talents through accelerated programs. On the whole, the Canadian model is rock solid precollege preparation, and it is made possible because Canadian mathematics education takes advantage of the enriching negative number environment provided by the Celsius scale.

Unfortunately, the newly implemented Common Core State Standards (CCSS) mathematics curriculum does nothing to address the issue of an early start with negative numbers. Grades 1 through 5 contains the same old set of concepts dressed up in fine-sounding language, infused with a great number of confusing and frustrating exercises for students and teachers alike. With few exceptions, the focus is exclusively limited to the four basic operations with whole numbers, fractions, and decimals. Here are CCSS standards for the fifth grade:

Mathematics | Grade 5
In Grade 5, instructional time should focus on three
critical areas: (1) developing fluency with addition and
subtraction of fractions, and developing understanding of
the multiplication of fractions and of division of fractions
in limited cases (unit fractions divided by whole numbers
and whole numbers divided by unit fractions); (2) extending
division to 2-digit divisors, integrating decimal fractions
into the place value system and developing understanding
of operations with decimals to hundredths, and developing
fluency with whole number and decimal operations; and (3)
developing understanding of volume.[71]

Thus the CCSS "Grade 5" curriculum continues the same old practice of beating these concepts to death for the first five years in the lives of elementary school students. If we take kindergarten into account, this is a waste of six years, spent only on whole numbers, fractions, and decimals, without once mentioning the rich universe of negative numbers on the left side of the number line.

Regarding an introduction to negative numbers, CCSS does exactly as was done before, in that they are introduced in the 6th grade. The CCSS Standard for the 6th grade is as follows:

Mathematics | Grade 6
In Grade 6, instructional time should focus on four critical
areas: (1) connecting ratio and rate to whole number
multiplication and division and using concepts of ratio and

*rate to solve problems; (2) completing understanding of
division of fractions and extending the notion of number
to the system of rational numbers, which includes negative
numbers; (3) writing, interpreting, and using expressions
and equations; and (4) developing understanding of
statistical thinking.[72]*

Regarding the issue of signed numbers to prepare students for algebra, nothing has changed fundamentally in the CCSS. It will be shown later that instead of expanding topics, the CCSS has truncated the old NTCM standards to focus on fewer topics. In chapter 9, we will show that the truncation was due to the hurried nature of constructing the CCSS. We will also show how the NCTM views with skepticism the structure, language, and legitimacy of the CCSS.

In this chapter, we have looked at the elements of the K–12 mathematics curriculum as it relates to a lack of exposure to negative numbers before the sixth grade. Attention was focused on the fact that there is no environmental supporting resource that would enable an earlier start with algebra. We have also seen that the CCSS curriculum provides no improvement. In the next chapter, our aim is to explore the permanent fix. For this, we will compare the number systems of the Celsius and Fahrenheit scales and point out why one is the solution, while the other is a perpetuation of what I would refer to as the "PISA problem," meaning the persistent trending down of the performance of US fifteen-year-old students on the PISA mathematics and science tests.

CHAPTER 5:
Why Celsius and not Fahrenheit for Mathematics Education?

5.1 The Numeration Systems of the Celsius Scale vs. the Fahrenheit Scale

As a mathematics teacher, I've always been on keen alert throughout my waking hours for situations outside the classroom environment that could enhance the teaching/learning process

One February morning in 2015, in Pennsylvania, I saw a school bus filled with children on its way to an elementary school. The bus passed by a large billboard showing a temperature of 9°F. I checked the weather app on my cell phone, which has readings in both scales, and saw that it was −14°C. It occurred to me that a similar busload of elementary school students in Canada on their way to school passing a similar billboard, with the same temperature, would see the negative number reading of −14, on the Celsius scale. I must confess to feeling a sense of despair for the students on that school bus. This was an algebraic moment par excellence, and those American students missed it. More disconcertingly, they had been continuously deprived of such algebraic moments since birth. If they were first graders, they would miss it for the next five years. If they were fifth graders, they had been missing this cognitive resource every winter day since they were born. This has been happening all across our country, where only Fahrenheit readings are available, with positive numbers for subfreezing temperatures. On that morning I was disgusted with Fahrenheit. What purpose does it serve, I asked myself, other than an unnecessary encumbrance to an early start in algebra? This temperature reading, which is out of step with the rest of the world, was repeated several times on my car radio. On arriving home, the cable Weather Channel, as seen in Pennsylvania, had the same local positive Fahrenheit reading, with five-day projections of daily high and low temperatures, all subfreezing and all positive numbers. This year, the 2014–2015 winter was particularly rich in subfreezing temperature readings (all negative numbers in Celsius) in the Northeast of our country. What a waste of an available resource! That day, the fact that my country, the United States, placed thirtieth in the world in mathematics on the 2012 PISA test, loomed largely on my mind.

In this chapter, we'll get to the essence of how using the Celsius scale can revolutionize mathematics education in this country, beginning at the prekindergarten level. We'll demonstrate the nature of Celsius, the inherent beauty and symmetry of its numeration system, and the potent mathematical resource it will provide in the daily lives of young children. We'll show that children will be living and adapting to the negative numbers of Celsius, not as an abstraction in a classroom, but as a necessary daily advisory utility during the winter months. The overarching superiority and aesthetics of the Celsius numeration system, when compared to the Fahrenheit Scale, will attest to the value-added asset of Celsius. There will be specific illustrations as to how the numeration system of the former enhances mathematics education, and it will be shown in precise terms that continuing inculcation with Fahrenheit and its asymmetric number distribution maintains the ignorance of negative numbers, particularly in the K–6 range of our educational system. It is the prekindergarten immersion in the Celsius numeration system and its inherent patterns that facilitates the early starting of algebra in the K–6 span of the mathematics curriculum in countries like Russia and allows Canadian students to complete calculus in the twelfth grade, as specified in their curriculum. The prekindergarten immersion in a Celsius environment would lead to the precollege preparation that would allow the US to be second to none in the world. This is the preparation our fifteen-year-old students will need, not only when they show up at the PISA test, but to be provided with a strong precollege mathematics preparation. These same students will increase the number of mathematics, science, and engineering science graduates from our universities, thus alleviating the need to import and to hire foreign-born talent in these subjects.

A mandatory and necessary change in measurements systems does not have to be precipitous or arbitrary; it should be well planned through convenient and constructive phasing-in initiatives. This process will be discussed in chapter 7.

To begin our comparison of temperature measurements systems, let us observe a side-by-side chart containing the Fahrenheit (°F) and the Celsius (°C) scales on either sides of a thermometer in figure 5.1. It shows comparative readings in the same selected temperature range in both scales.[73]

The Fahrenheit scale was developed by the German-Dutch physicist Gabriel Daniel Fahrenheit in 1724. It was based on two reference temperatures, namely, the melting point and boiling point of water. It is arbitrarily divided into 180 equal intervals or degrees. The boiling point was taken as 212°F, and the freezing (melting) point was taken as 32°F.[74]

The Celsius Scale, on the other hand, was later developed by Anders Celsius, a Swedish mathematician, astronomer, and physicist, in 1742.[75] He deliberately used 0°C as the freezing point of water and 100°C as the boiling point. It is sometimes called "centigrade" because there were 100 units between the freezing and boiling points of water. The scale was established as an international standard and is "still used in almost all scientific work."[76]

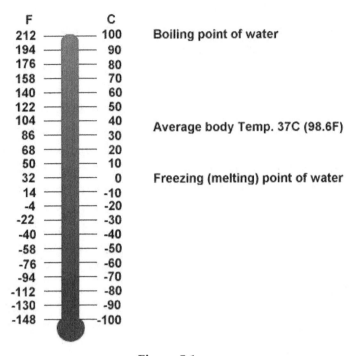

F	C	
212	100	Boiling point of water
194	90	
176	80	
158	70	
140	60	
122	50	
104	40	
86	30	Average body Temp. 37C (98.6F)
68	20	
50	10	
32	0	Freezing (melting) point of water
14	-10	
-4	-20	
-22	-30	
-40	-40	
-58	-50	
-76	-60	
-94	-70	
-112	-80	
-130	-90	
-148	-100	

Figure 5.1

As shown in figure 5.1, this representation of the Fahrenheit scale (°F) does not include the mathematically important number that is zero. This is because zero is neither a significant nor a critical point on the Fahrenheit scale. In short, 0°F (which is −17°C is just another subfreezing temperature. Fahrenheit has the freezing (melting) point of water as 32 degrees. The Celsius scale (°C), on the other hand, has the number zero representing the critical point where water begins to freeze or ice begins to melt, and is in synchrony with the number line, where zero is the critical point separating positive from negative numbers.

The number zero occupies a unique place in mathematics. I've previously mentioned that division by zero is not allowed. A search on any bookselling website will show that there are several books written about zero. My favorite is one entitled *Zero: The Biography of a Dangerous Number*. The first chapter, "Chapter 0," is entitled "Null and Void," and it begins with the following statement: "Zero hit the USS *Yorktown* like a torpedo. On September 21, 1997, while cruising off the coast of Virginia, the billion dollar missile cruiser shuddered to a halt. Yorktown was dead in the water."[77]

What was it that shut down the *USS Yorktown*? The book went on to explain: "When the *Yorktown*'s computer system tried to divide by zero, 80,000 horsepower instantly became worthless."[78]

Of the four basic operations (addition, subtraction, multiplication, and division) in mathematics, binary operations can be done on any two numbers except in division. We can add any two numbers, we can subtract any two numbers, we can multiply any two numbers, but with division, there is an exception. We can divide by any number—except zero. Try it for yourself on a calculator. If you divide any number by zero, you will get a response such as, "Cannot divide by zero." Since division by zero is considered "undefined," in mathematics, it will show up as an error in calculations or in computer programs. This was the case with the *USS Yorktown* story, but the book goes on to elaborate on the historical intrigues and importance of zero:

> *No other number can do such damage. Computer failures like the one that struck the Yorktown are just a faint shadow of the power of zero. Cultures girded themselves against zero, and philosophies crumble under its influence, for zero is different from all other numbers. It provides a glimpse of the ineffable and the infinite. This is why it has been feared and hated—and outlawed.*[79]

I would recommend that every parent, teacher, and student read this book.

In spite of the mathematical significance of zero in the history of mathematics, when Daniel Fahrenheit created his scale in 1724, he completely ignored its uniqueness and made it a mundane reading point on the Fahrenheit scale, where, as just another subfreezing temperature, it has no critical significance. On the other hand, when Anders Celsius created his scale, the evidence suggests that he knew that zero was a critical number for mathematics.

In chapter 3, you were asked to keep the number line in mind, even if you did not understand some parts of that chapter. In the next chart, figure 5.2, it will become clear why I made that request. The figure shows a three-column chart of a corresponding range of numbers using segments of the Fahrenheit scale, the Celsius scale, and the real number line.

Fahrenheit Scale (°F)	Celsius Scale (°C)	Number Line Integers
+50	+10	+10
+48	+9	+9
+46	+8	+8
+45	+7	+7
+43	+6	+6
+41	+5	+5
+39	+4	+4
+37	+3	+3
+36	+2	+2
+34	+1	+1
+32	0	0
+30	-1	-1
+28	-2	-2
+27	-3	-3
+25	-4	-4
+23	-5	-5
+21	-6	-6
+19	-7	-7
+18	-8	-8
+16	-9	-9
+14	-10	-10

Figure 5.2: *Segmental Alignment the Fahrenheit and Celsius Scales, and the Number Line*

As can be observed, the Celsius scale, as used in the international community, matches perfectly with the numbers of the number line used in beginning algebra. The same cannot be said about the Fahrenheit scale. As we would say in mathematics, the Fahrenheit scale, as it relates to temperature readings, is numerically incongruous with the number line. In short, in Celsius readings, the words "subfreezing," and "subzero" are synonymous and are thus negative. As can also be seen, this is not the case with the Fahrenheit scale, where the subfreezing temperatures between 0 and 32 degrees are all positive.

The crucial point being made here is that making the Celsius (°C) scale a part of the daily lives of young preschool and elementary school children, as is the case in other metric system countries, will provide them with one of the most powerful intuitive tools for mathematics. It would make them "integer ready"[80] for mathematics in general and beginning algebra in particular before entering kindergarten. It would make the suggestion by the mathematics teachers to the NMAP that there should be "More focus on positive vs. negative numbers" unnecessary, because such numbers would already be a natural part of students' world.

The statement "Give me the child until he is [age] seven and I'll give you the man," is an old saying attributed to St. Francis Xavier.[81] This encapsulates the fact that the character and learning profile of a person is directly related to learning influences between birth and the age of seven. When the living environment of young children contains the ingredients for learning, it has an enriching cognitive impact on their preparation for school.

Most radio stations report temperature readings every hour throughout the day. All local TV news broadcasts give high and low temperature readings several times daily. The metric chart—figure 1.2 in chapter 2—shows that Jamaica went on the metric system in 1998. Since then, all temperature readings announced on radio or television are reported in both Fahrenheit and Celsius as a process of transitioning from the former to the latter. Unfortunately for Jamaican children (even though fortunately for tourists), it is very unlikely that they will experience negative numbers during winter. However, as we have seen, the Celsius thermometer or chart in their classrooms will match perfectly with the number line.

As opposed to Jamaica, we in the United States have a veritable intuitive gold mine in winter temperatures, but we have no opportunity to mine this vital educational resource of negative numbers because of the continued use of the Fahrenheit scale. My distressful experience with the negative number deprivation of the elementary school students in Pennsylvania led me to the next chart, figure 5.3. It will be shown beyond doubt why continued use of the Fahrenheit scale is a continuing encumbrance for mathematics and science education in the United States. The data on this chart shows the average winter temperatures for several states in the Unites States over the range of nineteen years from 1971 to 2000. Note that there is not a single negative average temperature on the Fahrenheit scale over the selected period for the winter months of December, January, and February.

| Winter Average | | State | Dec. | Jan. | Feb. |
°F	°C		(°F)	(°F)	(°F)
2.6	-16	Alaska	4	1	3
25.8	-3.4	Colorado	25	24	28
28.5	-1.9	Connecticut	31	26	28
25.4	-2.7	Idaho	24	24	28
28.3	-2.1	Illinois	30	25	30
29.4	-1.4	Indiana	31	26	31
21.7	-5.7	Iowa	23	18	24
31.9	-0.1	Kansas	32	29	35
16.8	-8.4	Maine	20	14	17
27.4	-2.6	Massachusetts	30	25	27
21.7	-2.6	Michigan	25	19	21
21.2	-6.0	Montana	21	18	24
21.1	-6.1	New Hampshire	24	18	21
23.3	-4.8	New York	27	21	23
12.2	-11.0	North Dakota	13	8	15
28.4	-2.0	Pennsylvania	31	26	28
31.4	-0.3	Rhode Island	34	29	31
19.8	-6.9	South Dakota	20	16	23
28.2	-2.1	Utah	27	26	32
19.4	-7.0	Vermont	23	16	19
17.2	-8.2	Wisconsin	19	13	19
21.1	-6.0	Wyoming	21	19	24

Figure 5.3, Average Winter Temperatures for 22 States (1971-1990):
Source: http://www.currentresults.com/Weather/US/average-state-temperatures-in-winter.php

On the other hand, note that the Celsius average for every winter was negative. Please also note that, with one or two exceptions, the temperatures for December, January, and February are all below 32 degrees on the Fahrenheit scale and would all be negative in a Celsius environment.

So here is a case where American students in the states listed lived through decades with little or no experience in negative temperature readings, even though most days in the three winter months had subfreezing temperatures. In short, our American children had a negative number deprivation for all those nineteen years, and nothing has changed since. Schoolchildren must wait until the sixth grade before learning about negative numbers in classrooms, and only in classrooms. Under the Common Core Standards, they will continue to get the first notion of negative numbers in grade 6. As alluded to before, after learning of the existence this new category of numbers in the classroom, there is no resource in the regular cultural environment to make negative numbers real and to provide cognitive reinforcement.

It is known beyond doubt that young children have a "genetic propensity to learn language."[82] Those who grow up in a particular language environment, for example, tend to do better at learning that language than those people who start studying it at a later age. The language of mathematics is the real number system. Since the Celsius scale has congruence with a critical segment of the real number system, the earlier we can immerse children in that environment, the more effective will be the learning outcomes in mathematics and in science. This has more efficacy than the suggestion of the NMAP report to assign "harder problems."

This idea of assigning "harder problems" reminds me of the "drill and kill"[83] concept proposed by a few misguided mathematics educators, who confuse unnecessarily difficult problems, which lead to frustration, lethargy, and boredom, with the excitement of problems that are easy yet challenging and psychologically rewarding. The notion of "harder problems" is relative. If by the word "harder" they mean "challenging," most mathematics teachers know that "challenging" problems becomes less challenging when students have the required prerequisite knowledge. The "drill and kill" methodology is sometimes seized on by politicians who know very little about pedagogy but use the frustration of parents to propose costly changes like lengthening the school day and the school year.

The use of Celsius in the United States will pay conceptual dividends beyond mathematics. When children experience both negative and positive numbers at an early age, seven days per week, during their waking hours, during the three winter months every year, their young minds will be conditioned with the keys to understanding not only mathematics but some of the basic laws of science in general, and chemistry, biology, and physics in particular.

The basic constituent of matter is the atom. It consists of varying combinations of electrons, each with a negative charge; protons, each with a positive charge; and neutrons, each with a zero charge.

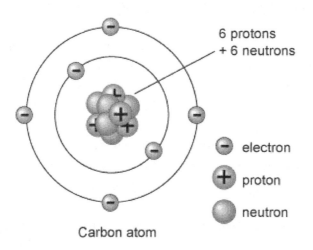

Carbon atom

Figure 5.5: *Source: http://www.universetoday.com/82128/parts-of-an-atom/*

The diagram in figure 5.5 shows the constituents parts of a carbon atom, with the nucleus consisting of 6 protons and 6 neutrons. As indicated, each proton has a positive charge, and each neutron has a zero charge. The two outer concentric circles are called electron shells, and that is where the negatively charged electrons are located. In the standard model of the atom, the innermost shell can accommodate no more than 2 electrons, while the next orbit can have no more than 8. The carbon atom, as can be seen here, can accommodate 4 more electrons in its outer shell, and that situation makes it easy to combine with other atoms, including other carbon atoms, which also "need" 8 electrons in the second shell. But the atom itself has a net charge of zero, because the 6 protons, all positively charged, are balanced by the 6 electrons, which are all negatively charged.

You may find it interesting to go to the Internet and explore how one oxygen atom, which has 8 protons and 8 electrons, attracts 2 hydrogen atoms, each with one proton and one electron and combine to form one molecule of water. Atoms are the basic unit of all the elements in the universe. Particle physics and quantum mechanics begin with the atom and the investigation of its inner forces and constituent particles.

The lesson to be learned from the carbon atom, illustrated in figure 5.5, or any other elements in the periodic chart of the elements, is that the Celsius scale, with both positive and negative numbers, will provide young children with basic concepts for not only for an early start in mathematics, but will prepare them to go beyond, to understanding the fundamentals and basic characteristics of the constituents of matter in the Universe.

5.2 Early Introduction to Algebra in a Celsius Environment

In this section we'll discuss how, in a Celsius environment, experiential acquaintance with negative as well as positive numbers can facilitate an early introduction to algebra.

In the history mathematics, whenever a set of numbers was discovered or defined, the first undertaking was to establish how to perform the four basic operations, i.e., how to add, subtract, multiply, and divide such numbers. In the Roman numeral system, for example, these four operations were very difficult because, for one thing, there is no zero in that system.

The mathematics in elementary school in this country starts with the whole numbers and the four basic operations. Children learn that if we add any two whole numbers, we get a whole number answer. For example, 5 + 2 = 7. The same principle applies with multiplication; for example, $5 \times 2 = 10$. Order is not important for addition or multiplication, and in mathematics we call this the commutative property. For example, $5 + 2 = 2 + 5$, and $5 \times 2 = 2 \times 5$. So in essence, addition and multiplication are commutative operations. Subtraction and division, however, are not commutative. In division and subtraction, order is important. In division, $8 \div 2$ is not the same as $2 \div 8$. In subtraction, $6 - 2 = 4$, but there is no whole number answer for $2 - 6$. In other words, we cannot subtract 6 from 2 in a whole number environment.

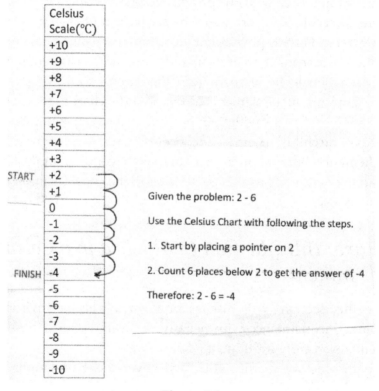

Figure 5.6

In a Celsius environment, however, where we have the integers, which include negative numbers, there is an answer to $2 - 6$. For example, if the Celsius temperature at a certain point in time is 2 degrees, and later the temperature falls 6 degrees, we have a new reading of –4 degrees. Thus the subtraction problem $2 - 6$, which has no whole number answer in the American elementary school, does have an answer of −4 in countries that have the Celsius scale, which goes beyond whole numbers to include negative numbers. In other words, a second- or third-grade student in a Celsius environment would know intuitively that if the temperature reading at a particular moment was 2 degrees, and later fell 6 degrees, the new reading would be −4 degrees. The intuitive nature of this solution can be bolstered with the exercise illustrated in figure 5.6.

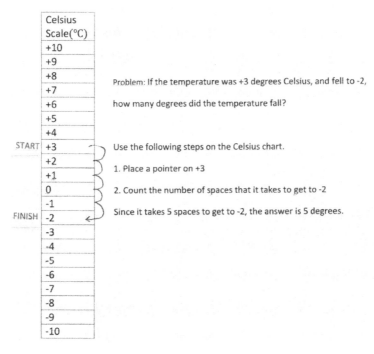

Figure 5.7

This exercise, with answer −4, is similar to the subtraction problem (+2) − (+6), which can be found in ninth-grade textbooks in beginning algebra across the US, or in developmental mathematics courses at community colleges. With exercises such as this, elementary school students can begin to develop cognition of subtraction involving two numbers with unlike signs.

Consider another subtraction problem (+3) − (−2), which can be found in a ninth grade textbook in beginning algebra. Third graders in the US could not do this subtraction, because they rarely if ever see a negative number. However, in a Celsius environment the subtraction can easily be done by asking any third grader the question, "If the temperature was +3 degrees and fell to −2, how many degrees did the temperature fall?" Figure 5.7 illustrates how that third grader could physically count the answer, by putting a pointer on +3 on a Celsius thermometer chart (which as we have seen is the same as the number line) and physically count the spaces (degrees) taken to lower the temperature to −2, to get an answer of 5 degrees.

This kind of exercise is a precursor for discovering the rule of subtraction inherent in the equivalent algebra problem (+3) − (−2), whose answer is 5. Note that (+3) − (−2) has the same answer as (+3) + (+2), which is also 5. This observation conforms to the rule of subtraction, which is: to subtract a number is the same as adding the opposite of the number being subtracted. (More will be said about the subtraction proposition in a later chapter.) In this problem, the opposite of −2 is +2. This vividly illustrates that this type of problem does not have to wait until the eighth or ninth grade, as is the current practice in our Fahrenheit environment.

In this country, students in the ninth grade are almost at age fifteen. To have students starting algebra this late is one of the great shortcomings in the American mathematics curriculum. To repeat the rhetorical question; is it any wonder why the American fifteen-year-old students placed thirtieth in the world on the PISA test in 2012?

5.3 How the Canadian Curriculum Exploits Celsius for Mathematics Education

As previously stated, Canada, a metric system country, has never fallen below the top ten on the PISA test. It is instructive to look at a relevant part of the Canadian mathematics curriculum, where acquaintance with negative numbers begins with prekindergarten awareness. Here is one of the "Specific Expectations" for the fifth grade:

> *measure and record temperatures to determine and represent*
> *temperature changes over time (e.g., record temperature*

changes in an experiment or over a season)
(**Sample problem**: *Investigate the relationship between weather, climate, and temperature changes over time in different locations.);*[84]

In the Canadian seventh grade, one of the "Overall Expectations" is as follows:

By the end of the 7th grade, students will:
demonstrate an understanding of addition and subtraction of fractions and integers, and apply a variety of computational strategies to solve problems involving whole numbers and decimal numbers;[85]

And the "Specific Expectation" is as follows:

– identify and compare integers found in real-life contexts (e.g., –10°C is much colder than +5°C);
– represent and order integers, using a variety of tools (e.g., two-color counters, virtual manipulatives, number lines);[86]

There are two elements in the expectations to be noted. These temperatures consist of the negative and positive numbers, and the assignment is practicable in the Canadian Celsius environment. In Canada, the infusion of temperatures in the mathematics curriculum in early grades makes it clear that the Celsius scale is used as a specific resource for mathematics education. If an American student did the same "real life" assignment, the two temperatures given in the example would be both positive, because –10°C in Canada is equivalent to +14°F in the United States. You will also note the reference to "number lines," the concept I requested that you keep in mind. This part of the Canadian mathematics curriculum really gets to the heart of what this letter is about in general and specifically what is wrong with mathematics education in the United States. In Postscript #4, I will be discussing how to use the "two-color" counters mentioned in the Canadian "Specific Expectation." Now let's take a look at an exercise in the Canadian curriculum.

Day 1 Sun. +15°	
Day 2 Mon. +12°	1. What is the difference between the
Day 3 Tue. +9°	highest and the lowest tempera-
Day 4 Wed. +6°	tures?
Day 5 Thurs. +3°	2. What are the average temperatures
Day 6 Fri. 0°	for the
Day 7 Sat. -3°	a. First Week?
Day 8 Sun. -6°	b. The second week?
Day 9 Mon. -9°	c. The 15 days?
Day 10 Tue. -12°	3. Which day was 18° warmer than
Day 11 Wed. -15°	Wed. the 11th day?
Day 12 Thurs. -18°	
Day 13 Fri. -21°	
Day 14 Sat. -24°	
Day 15 Sun. -27°	

Figure 5.8: *Source: New York City Math Project, Lehman College, New York.*

In figure 5.8 we have an assignment that was given in the Klondike schools in Canada. The assignment was that the students should keep a record of the temperatures for fifteen days, as seen on the left side of the chart. At the end of fifteen days, each student had to do the calculations on the right side. Note that the operations involved were subtraction, addition, and division. Taking averages involves addition and division. Here is a case where a real-life situation, as mentioned in the Canadian "Specific Expectation" above was integrated into classroom activities. In the US, students in the seventh grade could not get the full benefit from such an assignment because temperatures above the −18°C reading on Day 12 would all be positive on the Fahrenheit scale, and the critical point 0°C on the Celsius scale would be 32°F in the United States.

Any mathematics teacher will tell you that the above assignment is solid preparation for algebra, particularly for solving simple equations. It put Canadian children several years ahead of their US counterparts. We will never see significant improvement unless we start algebra in much earlier grades than is the current practice. That is why the teachers suggested to the NMAP that there should be "more focus on positive vs. negative numbers."

5.4 Starting Signed Number Operations before the Sixth Grade

We have suggested that addition and subtraction of signed numbers, restricted to integers, can be taught in the third grade in a Celsius environment. But how about multiplication and division in the same environment? I believe that were we to convert to Celsius, we should immediately pilot a program based on the following goal: reconstruct the grade 6 mathematics curriculum of the NTCM standards, spelling out the expectation that by the end of the fifth grade, all students should be able to add, subtract, multiply, and divide integers (signed numbers).

Students entering grade 6 in a Celsius environment should have mastered addition and subtraction of signed numbers. With mastery of addition, it is easy to transition to multiplication. Students should be expected to learn the two propositions on the binary operations of multiplication, i.e., multiplying two integers with like signs, and multiplying two integers with unlike signs. Preparation should begin with establishing certain conventional norms involving the commutative property of multiplication. For example, we can write the multiplication of say, 3 and 4 in several ways—such as 3×4, 4×3, (3)(4), 3(4), (3)4, 3*4, 4*3—or we can verbally state, find the product of 3 and 4. For algebra, it is conventional and convenient to use parentheses for multiplication, or to find products. For example, finding the product of 5 and 2 can be expressed as (5)(2) or (2)(5) to give an answer of 10.

As such, let us consider the following four multiplication examples as typical of what an America student in a Celsius environment should be able to master by the end of the fifth grade.

1. (+3)(+2)
2. (+3)(−2)
3. (−3)(+2)
4. (−3)(−2)

Although there are four problems, there are only two propositions for multiplication of signed numbers: multiplying two numbers with like signs and multiplying two numbers with unlike signs.

Let us apply an effective pedagogical approach to all four examples. Beginning with the simplest example, and using the Socratic method, which I like to refer to as the "ask-->elicit" paradigm, we proceed as follows:

1. We know that (+3)(+2) is the same as 3 × 2 = 6 or +6.
   Ask: Why is $3 \times 2 = 6$?
   Elicit: Since multiplication is a shortcut for adding the same number several times, 3×2 is the same as the addition problem 2 + 2 + 2, which gives 6 as the answer.

2. Discussing (+3)(−2).
   Ask: Using what we learned in 1, how can we express (+3)(−2) as an addition problem?
   Elicit: Since +3 can be written as 3, we can now write (+3)(−2) as 3(−2) or (−2) + (−2) + (−2).
   Ask: Using addition how can we find the answer to (+3)(−2)?
   Elicit: The answer is (−2) + (−2) + (−2) = −6

3. Discussing (−3)(+2). We can use the commutative property of multiplication to rewrite (−3)(+2) as (+2)(−3) or 2(−3) and use the method used in problem 2. Hence 2(−3) = (−3) + (−3) = −6.
   Ask: Relating to the sign of the answer, what observation did you make when we multiply two numbers with unlike signs?
   Elicit: The answer is negative.

4. Discussing (−3)(−2). Since both numbers are negative, deriving the answer mathematically may be somewhat challenging for the fifth grade. However, we can use a number of informal proofs or analogies based on logic. For example: Since the product of two signed numbers is either negative or positive, and since we learned that (−3)(+2) has a negative answer, which is −6, it makes sense that the product (−3)(−2) must have a different answer than −6, therefore the only alternative is that the answer must be +6. We can also use a verbal approach, with a sentence containing two negatives.
   Consider the statement: **The snake is alive**. We can negate this statement by inserting the word **not**. The new statement now reads: The snake is **not** alive. If we insert the word **not**

a second time, we are introducing a second negation and the statement would now read: The snake is **not** (**not** alive). Since (**not** alive) means dead, the statement could also be read, "The snake is **not** dead." Therefore, "The **snake is alive**." The two negations cancel out each other, and this brings us back to the original statement.

In summary, there are two propositions in the binary operation of multiplication of signed numbers.

> **Proposition 1**: *When multiplying two numbers with like signs, the answer is positive.*
> **Proposition 2**: *When multiplying two numbers with unlike signs, the answer is negative.*

The two propositions for division of two signed numbers have a similarity with multiplication.

Let's start with examples such as $\frac{6}{2} = 3$, because by using $2 \times 3 = 6$, we can derive the two propositions for division.

1. $\frac{+6}{+2} = +3$, because $(+2)(+3) = +6$

2. $\frac{-6}{-2} = +3$, because $(-2)(+3) = -6$

3. $\frac{-6}{+2} = -3$, because $(+2)(-3) = -6$

4. $\frac{+6}{-2} = -3$, because $(-2)(-3) = +6$

Parents can access the intricacies of the four operations of signed numbers from the Internet. The salient point is that children can master the basic operation of signed numbers by the end of the fifth grade if we have a Celsius environment, which is rich with negative and positive numbers. With this approach we could make a great leap forward in mathematics education.

5.5 *Consequences of Continuing with Fahrenheit*

Continuing to use Fahrenheit in this country has three distinct disadvantages for mathematics education. The first is that children must wait until the sixth grade, at best, to become familiar with negative numbers. The second is that learning about this new category of numbers only from lessons in classrooms with no environmental reinforcement makes them mere abstractions with no relevance to real life. The third is that the conjoining of the negative numbers with their positive counterparts without the readiness skills that are offered in the Celsius culture creates an unfamiliar set of numbers, producing confusion, especially for the middle- and lower-performing students, when the four basic operations of signed numbers are finally introduced sometimes as late as the ninth-grade level. As stated before, by the ninth grade, students are approaching age fifteen, the age for taking the PISA test. An American student coming from a Fahrenheit culture is conceptually and competitively dead on arrival at a PISA test.

As for the fifteen-year-old American students taking the PISA test, they will continue be outperformed by their international counterparts for decades to come. We already have the dreadful results for 2003, 2006, 2009, and 2012—with 2012 showing specific and dangerous decline with the worst results in mathematics since the PISA tests were implemented. Learning style is always an issue. As such, I will return to other approaches that parents can utilize to help children in learning these operations, in chapter 10 and in selected postscripts in PART V of this letter.

Practicing the four basic operations with only positive numbers reinforced by a Fahrenheit temperature environment creates a set of conditioned young minds with new necessities to relearn the rules of the four basic operations as they apply to signed numbers. As long as the Fahrenheit system remains in place, American fifteen-year-old students and adult students at the community college level will continue to be at a devastating disadvantage—not only in mathematics, but in science.

CHAPTER 6:

The Metric System as Facilitator for Science and Mathematics Education

In 2014, the Rosetta space probe that was launched in 2004 succeeded in landing a spacecraft on a comet in the solar system. Michael D. Lemonick wrote the following in *Scientific American*: "The 3000-kilogram robotic spacecraft launched by the European Space Agency was launched 10 years earlier and was en route to an August encounter with an obscure comet."[87]

From my experience in teaching about the metric system at various levels, very few Americans have an immediate grasp of what is meant by the weight "3000 kilograms." This is because the word "kilogram" belongs to the vocabulary of the metric system and is therefore not part of American utilitarian language of measurements. In this chapter, the intent is to delineate the characteristics of the metric system, to demonstrate its ease of use, and to describe its merits for laying the cognitive groundwork for American children engaged in science and mathematics education.

6.1 The Pure Metric System

The major attributes of the metric system are that it is decimalized (base ten), it is symmetrical, and it is aesthetically utilitarian. As previously indicated, it consists of three basic units of measure, i.e., the **meter**, the **gram**, and the **liter**. These three measures, excluding the Celsius scale, are what I refer to as the "pure metric system." It is more in line with our daily numerical system of numbers, because we live in a decimal culture. All the numbers we use in daily practice are in base ten. (I will explain "base ten" in section 6.2.) The fact that the metric system is consistent with the numbers we use in daily undertakings such as counting, purchasing, selling, and banking contributes to its ease of use and is a perfect match for our daily lives. For mathematics and science education, it has the numerical ingredients for early understanding of exponential expressions—both negative and positive—which is an enriching precursor to the upper-level mathematics concept called logarithms. It also engages the students in scientific notation, which also involves negative and positive numbers. The pure metric nomenclature contains key notations centered on one measure in each of three categories.

Unit of Measure	Equivalent in Meters	Exponential Form
1 kilometer	1000 meters	10^3 meters
1 hectometer*	100 meters	10^2 meters
1 dekameter*	10 meters	10^1 meters
1 meter	1 meter	10^0 meter
1 decimeter*	**0.1 meter**	**10^{-1} meter**
1 centimeter	0.01 meter	10^{-2} meter
1 millimeter	0.001 meter	10^{-3} meter

Figure 6.1: *Metric Units of Length*

In figure 6.1, we see the essence or partial listing of the nomenclature centered on the **meter**, the base unit for length. These are the only units needed in the early grades in schools for any measurements involving length. Each entry in the "Unit of Measure" column is either a multiple of a meter, the meter itself, or a sub-multiple of a meter. In the "Exponential Form" column, multiples have positive exponents, the central measure (the meter) has a zero exponent, and all submultiples have negative exponents.

With this in place, the metric system of weights can be easily constructed by merely replacing the word "meter" in figure 6.1 with the word "gram" to create the table in figure 6.2.

Unit of Measure	Equivalent in Grams	Exponential Form
1 kilogram	1000 grams	10^3 grams
1 hectogram*	100 grams	10^2 grams
1 dekagram*	10 grams	10^1 grams
1 gram	1 gram	10^0 gram
1 decigram*	**0.1 gram**	**10^{-1} gram**
1 centigram	0.01 gram	10^{-2} gram
1 milligram	0.001 gram	10^{-3} gram

Figure 6.2: *Metric Units of Weight*

In liquid measure or capacity, the same system is again reused by replacing the word "meter" in figure 6.1 with the word "liter" to create the table in figure 6.3.

Unit of Measure	Equivalent in Liters	Exponential Form
1 kiloliter	1000 liters	10^3 liters
1 hectoliter*	100 liters	10^2 liters
1 dekaliter*	10 liters	10^1 liters
1 liter	1 liter	10^0 liter
1 deciliter*	**0.1 liter**	**10^{-1} liter**
1 centiliter	0.01 liter	10^{-2} liter
1 milliliter	0.001 liter	10^{-3} liter

Figure 6.3: *Metric Units of Capacity*

These three tables of the pure metric system are the only ones needed for measurements in length, weight, and capacity for commerce and education beginning in kindergarten. The intrinsic simplicity, interchangeable arrangements, and ease of use of these measurements are characteristics that provide a powerful tool, with sophisticated mathematics made very simple. It provides a solid foundation for achieving excellence in mathematics and science education.

It must be noted that of the seven metric measures listed in each category, the three listed with asterisks contain prefixes that are merely placeholders and have very little utilitarian significance. There are very few instances, if any, where anyone in a metric culture is interested in measures beginning with the prefixes hecto, deka, or deci. For example, in the category containing the meter, the real-life utilitarian measures are the kilometer, the meter, the centimeter, and the millimeter. So in effect there are only four real-life utilitarian measures in each category. This characteristic of the metric system further contributes to its ease of use. For example, the great Jamaican athlete Usain Bolt, as the fastest man alive, has broken the one-hundred meter record. Now, one hundred meters is one hectometer, but the word "hectometer" is not a utilitarian part of the measurement nomenclature. It would sound a bit strange to say that "Usain Bolt is the fastest man to run a hectometer," even though the statement is true. History will record that, at this time, he is the fastest man to run one hundred meters.

Factor	Name	Symbol	Factor	Name	Symbol
10^{24}	yotta	Y	10^{-1}	deci	d
10^{21}	zetta	Z	10^{-2}	centi	c
10^{18}	exa	E	10^{-3}	milli	m
10^{15}	peta	P	10^{-6}	micro	μ
10^{12}	tera	T	10^{-9}	nano	n
10^{9}	giga	G	10^{-12}	pico	p
10^{6}	mega	M	10^{-15}	femto	f
10^{3}	kilo	k	10^{-18}	atto	a
10^{2}	hecto	h	10^{-21}	zepto	z
10^{1}	deka	da	10^{-24}	yocto	y

Figure 6.4: *Source: http://physics.nist.gov/cuu/Units/prefixes.html*

The prefixes indicating multiples or submultiples in the metric system are taken from the list of International System of Units (SI), as shown in Table 6.4 Those of you who are computer literate will recognize prefixes such as **mega**, as in **megabytes**, meaning millions of bytes of memory, and **giga** as in **gigabytes**, meaning trillions of similar bytes.

6.2 Base Ten System of Enumeration for Mathematics and Science

There is one very important concept that is fostered by the metric tables in figures 6.1, 6.2, and 6.3. You'll observe that the quantities in the third column are written with exponents using base ten. As mentioned before, multiples of a basic measure have positive exponents, the measure itself has a zero exponent, and all submultiples have negative exponents. The list of prefixes in table 6.4 has the same consistency. Thus, you can tell the prefixes representing multiples and those representing submultiples by looking at sign of the exponents. Your youngsters will learn that this way of representing numbers is very important for writing extremely large or extremely small numbers in a succinct form known as scientific notation.

Before getting to the use of scientific notation for large and small numbers, it is necessary to understand the intricacies of the base ten system in which we Americans live and work.

We in the United States, and in most if not all other countries, live in a **base ten** environment or base ten universe, in which the symmetric nature of the metric system is a nice and facilitating fit.

In base ten, there are only ten digits from which all numbers are formed. These ten digits belong to the digit set {0,1,2,3,4,5,6,7,8,9}. There are other bases than base ten. In computer science, for example, we have base two, consisting of the two digits in the digit set {0,1}. In a base five system, all the numbers consist of the five digits in the digit set {0,1,2,3,4}. To comprehend base ten fully, it is essential to understand how the digit sets of number bases are used to form numbers peculiar to that base. For this we will discuss the three bases: **base ten**, **base five**, and **base two**.

In a **base ten** universe like ours, all the numbers used in any enterprise are made up of numbers taken from the ten elements of the digit set {0,1,2,3,4,5,6,7,8,9}. If we started counting from 0, after getting to 9, in order to represent the next number, we must reach back into the digit set and select the digits **1** and **0**, in that order, to form the number we call "ten" or 10. By recursively adding 1 to each succeeding number, we get 11, then 12, 13, 14, and so on. When we get to 19, we must again reach back into the digit set to select the number 2 and 0, in that order, to form the number we call twenty or 20, and continue recursively with 21, 22, 23, 24, and so on, until we get to 29 and then reach back, as previously described, to get **3** and **0**, to form thirty or **30**, and so on.

The same principle applies to base five, which uses the digit set {0, 1, 2, 3, 4}. If we listed the first eleven numbers in base five we would get 0, 1, 2, 3, 4, 10, 11, 12, 13, 14, 20, and so on and so forth. This has a one-to-one correspondence with the base ten numbers 0, 1, 2, 3, 4, 5, 6, 7, 8, 9, 10. Note that the number called "five" in **base five** now takes the form **10**. In base five, we **cannot** use the word "**ten**" to characterize the number "**10**." In addition, the numerical symbols 5, 6, 7, 8, or 9 are not members of the **base five** digit set, and therefore cannot appear in any **base five** number.

Similarly, the base two digit set {0, 1} has only two numerical elements, which are **0** and **1**. A listing, in order, of the first nine numbers in **base two**, starting with zero, takes the form 0, 1, 10, 11, 100, 101, 110, 111, 1000. This corresponds in order to the base ten numbers 0, 1, 2, 3, 4, 5, 6, 7, 8, because the only digits that can appear in a base two number are 0 and 1. Here again is the same pattern of representing the **base number**. Note that the **base ten** number that is **2** is written as **10** in **base two**, and the base ten number **8** is now **1000** in **base two**, and again that's because only the numbers 0 and 1 can be used in base two. When your child studies number bases, he/she will be taught conversion methods between base ten and other bases and vice versa. By convention, in order to represent numbers in bases other than 10, we must specify the base. For example, 1000 in base two must be written as 1000_{two}. In like manner, the number 10 in base five must be written as 10_{five}. We do not specify the base in **base ten** numbers, because by convention when we write numbers without specifying the base, they are understood to be **base ten**.

Some scientific undertakings are made easier by using number bases other than **ten**. **Base two**, for example, facilitates computer language very nicely. By using the numbers **0** and **1** to represent an electronic switch in the **off** or **on** position respectively, the electronics of computer language becomes possible when combinations of switches are used. But that's computer science. I could easily get carried away with this fascinating part of mathematics or computer science. Let's get back to base ten, which is used in elementary school mathematics in this country, and how it fits very nicely with the metric system.

As stated previously, the number **ten** itself is formed by using the first two digits in the digit set. Thus we write the number "**ten**" as 10. Every subsequent counting number can be written using the base ten digits, even in with repeat of digits, such as the number 5555. We form the number 5555 by using the digit **5** four times.

You may recall the place value chart from elementary school. The numbers 9724 and 5555 fit into this chart as indicated in figure 6.5.

Thousands	Hundreds	Tens	Ones
9	7	2	4
5	5	5	5

Figure 6.5

In order to discover how base ten exponents are determined, let's revisit the metric charts in figures 6.1, 6.2, and 6.3. Without loss of generality, let's consider any one table, say figure 6.1, and consider the number 1000, which is represented by the word "kilo." 1000 can be expressed as multiples of 10. In other words, $1000 = 10 \times 10 \times 10$. We can then write 1000 as 10^3. As you will observe in all three metric charts, the prefix **kilo**, which represents 1000 is also expressed as 10^3. Hence we have the terms kilometer, kilogram, and kiloliter. Speaking of patterns, note the relationship between the number of zeros and the exponent in the following statement: We can write one thousand (1000) in exponential form as 10^3. (Note that the number **1** is followed by three zeros, thus the exponent is 3.)

Using the aforementioned pattern, we can write the number one million as $1,000,000 = 10^6$ because the number 1 is followed by 6 zeros. In this case we can verbally state that "**the number one million** is equal to **ten to the sixth power**." Where **1,000,000** is called the **number**, **10** is called the **base**, and **6** is called the **exponent**. We can also say that 1,000,000 is written in exponential form as 10^6. Continuing to use the pattern, we can use these relationships in reverse order to expand a number written in exponential form to get the number itself. For example: $10^4 = 10,000$, because the exponent 4 tells us that the number 1 is followed by 4 zeros. Observing this base ten pattern is another way of determining that $10^0 = 1$, because the **0** exponent tells us, by pattern, that there are no zeros after the number **1**.

We can now restructure the chart in figure 6.5 to take alternate form in figure 6.6 below. We can now rewrite 9724, in expanded form, as $9000 + 700 + 20 + 4$ or as $9 \times 1000 + 7 \times 100 + 2 \times 10 + 4 \times 1$; and this can be rewritten as $9 \times 10^3 + 7 \times 10^2 + 2 \times 10^1 + 4 \times 10^0$.

In like manner, we could write 5555 as $5 \times 10^3 + 5 \times 10^2 + 5 \times 10^1 + 5 \times 10^0$. So now, the two numbers 9724 and 5555 can fit into the chart as seen in figure 6.6:

10^3	10^2	10^1	10^0
9	7	2	4
5	5	5	5

Figure 6.6

You'll observe that the pattern of the descending order is another way of indicating that that 10^0 and the number **1** are equivalent. You'll see the same notation in the metric tables in figures 6.1, 6.2, and 6.3 for the **meter**, the **gram**, or the **liter**, respectively.

Base two and base five were mentioned above to give perspective to the notion of number base as a way to elucidate base ten. You may wonder how to convert 1000_{two} to base ten. If we take a look at figure 6.6, we could use a similar place value chart such as figure 6.7, using the number 2 as the base.

2^3	2^2	2^1	2^0
1	0	0	0
0	1	1	1

Figure 6.7

$1000_{two} = 1 \times 2^3 + 0 \times 2^2 + 0 \times 2^1 + 0 \times 2^0 = 1 \times 8 + 0 \times 4 + 0 \times 2 + 0 \times 1 = 8 + 0 + 0 + 0 = 8$.

Also, $0111_{two} = 0 \times 2^3 + 1 \times 2^2 + 1 \times 2^1 + 1 \times 2^0 = 0 \times 8 + 1 \times 4 + 1 \times 2 + 1 \times 1 = 0 + 4 + 2 + 1 = 7$.

Assuming that we now have some sense as to how number bases work, let's get back to base ten by proceeding to the list in figure 6.8, below, showing certain base ten numbers in three forms: numerical, fractional, and exponential. The fractional form is included to bring out a pattern that leads us to negative exponents. You will observe that pattern as we look at the fraction forms beginning with $100000 = \mathbf{10^5}$ and ending with the number $0.000001 = \mathbf{10^{-5}}$. Note also that the base ten exponents are listed in descending order, starting with 5 at the top of the chart, and ending with −5 at the bottom. Numbers greater than 1 have positive exponents, while numbers less than 1 but greater than zero have negative exponents.

The base ten system offers a convenient way to write very large or very small numbers in exponential form, otherwise called **scientific notation**.

For example, let's take the distance from the earth to the sun. The number is large whether expressed in USCS or metric units. In USCS the distance is 93,000,000 miles. In metric the distance is 300,000,000 kilometers.

We can write both quantities in scientific notation as follows:

1. 93,000,000 miles = 9.3×10^6 miles (note that 93,000,000 = $9.3 \times 1,000,000 = 9.3 \times 10^6$).

2. 300,000,000 km = 3×10^8 km (note that 300,000,000 = $3 \times 100,000,000 = 3 \times 10^8$).

NUMERICAL FORM	FRACTIONAL FORM	EXPONENTIAL FORM
100,000	$\dfrac{100000}{1}$	10^5
10,000	$\dfrac{10000}{1}$	10^4
1,000	$\dfrac{1000}{1}$	10^3
100	$\dfrac{100}{1}$	10^2
10	$\dfrac{10}{1}$	10^1
1	$\dfrac{1}{1}$	10^0
0.1	$\dfrac{1}{10}$	10^{-1}
0.01	$\dfrac{1}{100}$	10^{-2}
0.001	$\dfrac{1}{1000}$	10^{-3}
0.0001	$\dfrac{1}{10000}$	10^{-4}
0.00001	$\dfrac{1}{100000}$	10^{-5}

Figure 6.8: *Base Ten Numbers Written in Three Forms*

We have heard that the national debt of the United States was at one time approximately 19 trillion dollars, which in numerical terms is $19,000,000,000,000. But this very large number can be succinctly written in scientific notation as 1.9×10^{12}.

On the other hand, let's take an extremely small number used by scientists. The mass of a proton is 0.000000000000000000000000000168 kilogram. This submultiple of the kilogram is, relatively speaking, an extremely small number, but it is greater than zero. We can write the relationship between this number and its exponential form as follows: $0.000000000000000000000000000168 = 1.68\times10^{-27}$ kg. We have now written the mass of a proton in scientific notation: 1.68×10^{-27} kg.

A number written in **scientific notation** has the form $\mathbf{a} \times \mathbf{10^{n}}$; where $\mathbf{1 \leq a < 10}$. This requires that the number **a**, multiplying the base with its exponent **n**, must be greater than or equal to 1, and must be less than 10. (Please see Postscript #1 for an explanation of the inequality symbols ($<$, $>$, $\leq$, and $\geq$)).

For example, let's write 6700 in scientific notation. If we write 6700 as 67×10^2, it would be mathematically correct, but it would be incorrect as a number in scientific notation. Why? Because **67** is not less than **10**, and so $\mathbf{1 \leq 67 < 10}$ is a false statement, because it does not meet the criterion $\mathbf{1 \leq a < 10}$. The correct answer is 6.7×10^3. Why? Because 6.7 is less than 10, and so $\mathbf{1 \leq 6.7 < 10}$ is a true statement.

So now we know that in order to write a number in scientific notation, we must move the decimal point to a location where we have a number **a**, such that $\mathbf{1 \leq a < 10}$. To determine the exponent **n**, we count the number of places that we must move the decimal point to get to the number **a**. How do we decide the sign of the exponent? If we must count to the left, as is the case with the sun-to-earth distance, or the national debt, the exponent is positive. If we must count to the right, as is the case with the mass of the proton, the exponent is negative.

Note that the mass of a proton fits the inequality $0 < 6.8 \times 10^{-27} < 1$. This is because 6.8×10^{-27} is a number much smaller or less than 1, but greater than 0.

Students who are armed with the ability to write very large and very small numbers in scientific notation will have the ability to take on the study of the scientific properties of the universe from subatomic particles to the billions of stars and galaxies in the cosmos.

In this section, we have had an intricate explanation of how knowledge of base ten is essential for writing numbers of any magnitude in scientific notation. This was done to bring emphasis to point that early cultural as well as classroom immersion in the base ten structured metric system is what is needed for American schoolchildren to have a solid foundation for K–12 mathematics. As previously mentioned, every OECD country participating in the PISA test has the metric system. This provides their students with two magnificent readiness skills. One is the ability to perform on the PISA tests at a level commensurate with the money spent per student. The other is the acquisition of the necessary precollege readiness skills for excellence in mathematics, science, and engineering technology at the university level.

In the next section, we will dig a little deeper to demonstrate that while the numeration characteristics of metric system provide early acquaintance with the numbers needed for the study of science, the USCS offers only awkward accommodation in this domain.

6.3 The United States Customary System vs. The Metric System

In figure 2.3, in chapter 2, we showed a partial list of the measures used in the USCS. Let's revisit an isolated part of that list in figure 6.9, to get an in-depth sense of the awfully cluttered and difficult environment in which American children are forced to learn.

As was previously observed, by looking at the fourth column, each measure is expressed in one of the three the units of the metric system. In short, every US Customary measure has a metric equivalent in either meters, grams, or liters. These metric measures are essential elements of the language of scientific measurements.

The first three columns in the **CAPACITY** category have seven measures, namely: **gallon, quart, pint, gill, fluid ounce, fluid dram, and minim**. You'll observe that there is no pattern in the numerical relationship between these units, as is the case with the metric system. In addition, it is not a decimalized system. In the fourth or metric column, every single USCS measure ends with the word **liter**. In other words, all the USCS units of **capacity** can all be expressed either as liter, multiples of a liter, or submultiples of a liter. The same is true in the **LENGTH** category, which uses the **meter**, or the **WEIGHT** category, which uses the **gram**.

The USCS structure is not only lacking in interrelated names but lacks the esthetic beauty of patterns, and must be studied through the daunting task of memorizing each measurement as a distinct units. It illustrates in vivid terms the quagmire of measures that amounts to a pile of clutter in the mind and real life of the American student. It is unnecessary, and it encourages "drill and kill." In other words, it drills concepts and kills the joy, enthusiasm, and passion for mathematics.

CAPACITY			
US liquid measure			
gallon	gal	4 quarts (231 cubic inches)	3.785 liters
quart	qt	2 pints (57.75 cubic inches)	0.946 liter
pint	pt	4 gills (28.875 cubic inches)	473.176 milliliters
gill	gi	4 fluid ounces (7.219 cubic inches)	118.294 milliliters
fluid ounce	fl oz	8 fluid drams (1.805 cubic inches)	29.573 milliliters
fluid drams	fl dr	60 minims (0.226 cubic inch)	3.697 milliliters
minim	min	¹⁄₆₀ fluid dram (0.003760 cubic inch)	0.061610 milliliter
LENGTH			
mile	mi	5280 feet, 1760 yards, 320 rods	1.609 kilometers
rod	rd	5.5 yards, 16.5 feet	5.029 meters
yard	yd	3 feet, 36 inches	0.9144 meter
foot	ft *or* '	12 inches, 0.333 yard	30.48 centimeters
inch	in *or* "	0.083 foot, 0.028 yard	2.54 centimeters
WEIGHT			
short hundredweight		100 pounds, 0.05 short ton	45.359 kilograms
long hundredweight		112 pounds, 0.05 long ton	50.802 kilograms
pound	lb *or* lb avdp *also* #	16 ounces, 7000 grains	0.454 kilogram
ounce	oz *or* oz avdp	16 drams, 437.5 grains, 0.0625 pound	28.350 grams
dram	dr *or* dr avdp	27.344 grains, 0.0625 ounce	1.772 grams
grain	gr	0.037 dram, 0.002286 ounce	0.0648 gram

Figure 6.9

This is vivid illustration of the insightfulness of George Washington, who wanted the US to change to the metric system as early as the 1790s.

Let us take a look at a one example. Here, see the kind of problem children must be able to do in elementary school in the United States.

Subtract: (3 yards 2 feet 9 inches) from (6 yards 1 foot 5 inches).

This problems would be set up for subtraction as follows:

	6 yards	1 foot	5 inches
	3 yards	2 feet	9 inches
Answer:	2 yards	1 foot	8 inches

You'll observe that since this is not a decimalized (base ten) problem, we'll have to be very careful in converting from one measure to the next in order to get the correct answer. You can see the pen and paper calculations done in figure 6.10. The three steps taken to get the answer are written below:

1. We'll do the subtraction in the inch column. We cannot subtract 9 inches from 5 inches. Therefore, we must borrow 1 foot from the foot column, leaving 0 feet. But this borrowed foot must be converted to 12 inches in the inch column. The borrowed 12 inches are now added to the 5 inches we had before, and now we have 17 inches. Now we can subtract 9 inches from 17 inches to get 8 inches in the inch column.

2. Now we'll do the subtraction in the foot column. We are now required to subtract 2 feet from 0 feet, which cannot be done. Therefore, we must borrow 1 yard from the 6 yards in the yard column, leaving 5 yards. But this borrowed yard must now be converted to 3 feet since 1 yard = 3 feet. When the borrowed 3 feet is added to the 0 feet we had before, we now have 3 feet, from which we can subtract 2 feet to get 1 foot.

3. Now we'll do the subtraction in the yard column. We now subtract 3 yards from the 5 yards that was left to get 2 yards.

Combining steps 1, 2, and 3, we get the answer: 2 yards 1foot 8 inches as the answer.

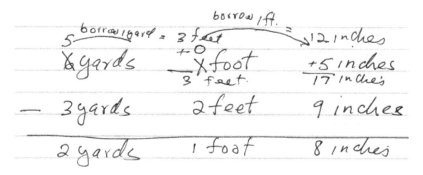

Figure 6.10

While US students are wasting time and being held back on such problems in classrooms in our country, similar students in Russia, Canada, Japan, Hong Kong, and Finland and all other countries that are continually ahead of the United States on the PISA test are engaged with problems such as the following.

Subtract: (3 meters 2 decimeters 9 centimeters) from (6 meters 1 decimeters 5 centimeters).

This problem can be set up for regular base ten subtraction as follows:

	6 meters	1 decimeters	5 centimeters
	3 meters	2 decimeters	9 centimeters
Answer:	2 meters	8 decimeters	6 centimeters

Since the metric system is base ten, this problem is no different from the regular base ten subtractions of whole numbers.

Hence we merely subtract 329 from 615 as indicated below.

$$
\begin{array}{r}
615 \\
-\ 329 \\
\hline
286
\end{array}
$$

This will give us the answer, 2 meters 8 decimeters 6 centimeters. Each time we borrow from the column on the left, we treat the borrowed number as **10**, thus making subtraction very easy in a metric system environment.

There does come a time in K–12 when students are required to have knowledge of the metric system, because it is a requirement for studying the sciences. By that time, the metric measures are presented to the students as new and unfamiliar concepts, because they have been acculturated to the USCS. Not only that, they have to be taught conversion methods between the two systems using charts like figure 6.11 (conversion from metric ton USCU), and figure 6.12 (conversion from USCS to metric).

Metric Units	Customary Units
1 centimeter	0.394 inch
1 meter	3.281 feet or 1.093 yards
1 kilometer	0.621 mile
1 gram	0.035 ounce
1 kilogram	2.205 pounds
1 milliliter	0.034 fuild ounce
1 liter	1.057 quart or 0.264 gallon

Figure 6.11: *Conversion from Metric to USCS Source: http://www. mathatube.com/*

I've taught the metric system as well as the mathematics of conversion from one system to the next at the community-college level, where several of my adult American students encountered metric measures for the first time. In fact, the metric measures are so foreign to these students that use of tables is allowed in tests and exams to facilitate questions involving conversions. If we were a metric country, we would be thinking in metric and working in metric and would have very little need for conversion tables. This gives emphasis to the point previously made, that thinking in USCS is truly damaging to math and science education. This is what was missed by the NMAP report, in spite of the fact that the mission was to report to President George W. Bush the best way to help students prepare for and succeed in algebra.

As is the case with negative numbers, while children of all ages in all the other industrialized countries grow up in a metric culture, adult students here in the US have little or no idea about these measures until they are taught in classrooms. After leaving the classroom, they return daily life into the USCS unit system with road signs in miles per hour, rather than kilometers per hour. A stop at the gas station reveals prices per gallon, rather than prices per liter. At the hardware store, all lengths are measures in feet or inches. With screws, drill bits, nuts, and bolts, we have fractions of an inch rather than meters, centimeters, or millimeters.

Customary Units	Metric Units
1 inch	2.54 centimeters
1 foot	30.48 centimeters
1 yard	0.914 meter
1 mile	1.609 kilometers
1 ounce	28.35 grams
1 pound	454 grams
1 fluid ounce	29.574 milliliters
1 quart	0.946 liter
1 gallon	3.785 liters

Figure 6.12: *Conversion from USCS to metric. Source: http://www. mathatube.com/*

If we intend to give our students the early preparation needed, not only for mathematics and engineering, but for chemistry, physics, biology, medicine, astronomy, and the geosciences, there is really no alternative for our children than for the United Sates to replace the cumbersome USCS with the metric system. This is the choice that must be made to ensure optimum precollege preparation. This is certainly one of the key missing elements of the CCSS.

CHAPTER 7:
Phasing in the Metric System: Not Only for Commerce but for Education

In chapter 2, we read that there is a history of recognition by the United States that predominant use of the metric system was in the best interest of the country, but only to facilitate international trade and commerce. That is why in the 1960s it fell to the Commerce Department to make recommendations for a change from USCS to metric. In fact, even now as I'm writing, there are significant segments of corporate and governmental activities in our country that utilize metric measurements. Most bottled, canned, and packaged products sold in the United States display both USCS and metric measurements. Others display only USCS measurements. The countrywide problem for education is that the mathematics and science curriculum in the early grades is still tied to the USCS. Children have to find areas and perimeters and volumes of geometric figures in inches,, feet, and yards instead of in meters and its multiples or submultiples. The net effect is that children, parents, and the population at large continue to think in USCS units such as yards (each of which is 36 inches), rather than in meters (each of which is 100 centimeters); gallons (each of which is 4 quarts, where one quart is 2 pints) instead of liters (each of which is 100 centiliters or 1000 milliliters); pounds (each of which is 16 ounces) instead of kilograms (each of which is 1000 grams). They continue to experience subfreezing weather but positive temperature readings, whereas children in the international community experience these same temperatures as negative numbers. The ramifications, as alluded to before, are that American K–12 students, needing to learn metric system concepts for mathematics and science, encounter these measures too late in the curriculum. Furthermore, they receive no reinforcing support in the regular culture, thus putting them at conceptual disadvantage. In effect, the challenges we face today where our students have demonstrated specific shortfalls in mathematics and science education are in a category that must be extended from a commerce/trade issue to an urgent educational issue.

What is now needed is a carefully planned implementation of the metric system to facilitate mathematics and science education in this country. It seems rational to conclude that an education problem should involve the Department of Education as the primary agent for change, and the solution must be an integral part of its mission. There are elements in the intersection of commerce and trade on one hand, and education on the other, that relate to change in measurements systems. Therefore, the US Department of Education can learn from the past, by revisiting the Commerce Department's initiative to effectuate that change.

According to the National Institute of Standards and Technology (NIST), in the late 1960s the Commerce Department, at the request of Congress, assembled a forty-five-member panel that "consulted with and took testimony from hundreds of consumers, business organizations, labor groups, manufacturers, and state and local officials."[88] The NIST went on to state that:

*The final report of the study, "**A Metric America: A Decision Whose Time Has Come,**" concluded that the U.S. would eventually join the rest of the world in the use of the metric system of measurement. The study found that measurement in the United States was already based on metric units in many areas and that it was becoming more so every day. The majority of study participants believed that conversion to the metric system was in the best interests of the nation, particularly in view of the importance of foreign trade and the increasing influence of technology in American life.[89]*

The NIST pointed out the most important recommendation for successful, pervasive, and permanent paradigm shift in measurement systems when it wrote that: "The study recommended that the United States implement a carefully planned transition to predominant use of the metric system over a ten year period."[90]

The reason we are not a metric system country here in the twenty-first century, in spite of our recognition of its efficacy from the 1800s through the 1980s, is because the Congressional "Metric Conversion Act of 1975" excluded a mandatory change and a ten- year phasing-in period. According to the NIST:

*Congress passed the **Metric Conversion Act of 1975** "to coordinate and plan the increasing use of the metric system in the United States." **The Act, however, did not require a ten year conversion period**. A process of voluntary conversion was initiated, and the U.S. Metric Board was established.[91]*

The historical perspective on the matter of measurement systems is instructive. We previously stated that our first president, George Washington, wanted to abandon the British system of measurement and replace it with the metric system. We also mentioned that President James Madison prompted Congress to act in like manner. But did you know that the United States was a signatory to the "Treaty of the Meter," as far back as 1875? The following informative and ostensibly hopeful statement is an excerpt from President Gerald Ford's prepared comments, when he signed the legislation for the **Metric Conversion Act of 1975:**

> *I am today signing H.R. 8674, the Metric Conversion Act of 1975. This legislation establishes a national policy of coordinating and planning for the increased use of the metric measurement system in the United States.*
>
> *To say that this legislation is historic is an understatement. The question of a common measurement language is, in fact, nearly as old as our country. President George Washington raised the issue in his first message to Congress on January 8, 1790. He called at that time for a uniform system of currency and weights and measures. He repeated his request several times thereafter.*
>
> *President James Madison also urged Congressional action on a measurement system. Fifty years later—in July 1866— Congress did pass legislation making it legal to use the metric system in U.S. trade and commerce.*
>
> *In 1875, the United States was one of the 17 countries which signed the Treaty of the Meter. In spite of that, the country retained its old measurement system. There have been expressions of legislative interest from time to time since 1875, but no further definitive statement of national policy has been forthcoming.*[92]

While President Ford's announcement encapsulated the various historical exhortations and the expressed urgency of the matter, his statement also contained the following unfortunate declaration:

> *It is important to stress that the conversion contemplated in this legislation is to be a completely voluntary one. The Government's function, through a U.S. Metric Board that I shall appoint, will be to coordinate and synchronize increasing use of metric measurement in the various sectors of our economy.*[93]

President Ford did indeed appoint the US Metric Board, but it was unable to accomplish the essential elements of its charge, stated as follows: "Devising and carrying out a broad program of planning, coordination, and public education, consistent with other national policy and interests, with the aim of implementing the policy set forth in this Act."[94]

Making the change of measurement systems voluntary rather than mandatory led to the ultimate demise of the Metric Board. According to the NIST:

> *The efforts of the Metric Board were largely ignored by the American public, and, in 1981, the Board reported to Congress that it lacked the clear Congressional mandate necessary to bring about national conversion. Due to this apparent ineffectiveness, and in an effort to reduce Federal spending, the Metric Board was disestablished in the fall of 1982.*[95]

The failure to include the ten-year phasing period is the specific culprit in our failure to change measurement systems. In 1980, as part of the voluntary effort to change to metric, gas stations around the country suddenly and without warning changed gallons to liters, and of course with a different pricing structure. In an article entitled "Half gallon liters: confusion at the gas pump," Gil Klein wrote the following in the *Christian Science Monitor*:

> *Everybody knows what a gallon is. They know how far a car can run on one. And, all things being equal, Americans doubtless would prefer to keep buying their gasoline in gallons—but few know what a liter is.*[96]

How would you like to purchase gas in gallons one day at a price and measure you understand, only to return to the same gas station a few days later, having to purchase gas at a new price in a measure called liters, when you have no idea what a liter is? My imagination tells me that the average American would exclaim, "What the hell is a liter?" According to Erin Condon, in her article "Still a Matter of Inches,"[97] the American public had a visceral resistance to such "foreign system" as road signs in kilometers, liters at the gas pump, and temperatures in Celsius. A barrage of constituents writing to their representatives in Congress doomed the US Metric Board. President Reagan disbanded it in 1982.

My take on the matter is that if Americans were informed that the change to the metric system is primarily to improve mathematics and science education, with ancillary effects in trade and commerce, they would be more accepting and would be willing participants in a constructive phasing-in process over a psychologically suitable period of time.

As the saying goes, hindsight is always 20/20. It would be easy to conclude that there was a dearth of leadership on the matter at the presidential level. It had the appearance that with incisive leadership, reaching out to seek advice from professionals in the educational community, we could have had a presidential address to the nation strengthening the US Metric Board, rather than a presidential disestablishment of its existence. But this may be unfair to President Ronald Reagan. Presidents of the United States are as good as their cabinet advisors. In foreign policy, for example, former Secretaries of State Henry Kissinger and James Baker were quintessential Presidential advisors. Kissinger was instrumental in opening relations between the US and China under President Nixon, and Baker worked to promote and adjust US policy in response to the monumental demise of the Soviet Union under George H. W. Bush.

It is now clear that President Ford was either ill advised or had no constructive guidance on the change in measurement systems when he gave specific assurance that the change would be voluntary rather than mandatory. The ten-year phasing-in period, recommended by the 1968 Commerce Department Report and Maurice Stans, was summarily ignored.

It is worth noting that President Gerald Ford had no secretary of education, because at that time there was no Education Department (ED). Education was under the umbrella of the Department of Health, Education, and Welfare. In 1980 there was a significant change:

In 1980, Congress established the Department of Education
as a Cabinet level agency. Today, ED operates programs that
touch on every area and level of education. The Department's

elementary and secondary programs annually serve nearly 14,000 school districts and some 56 million students attending roughly 99,000 public schools and 34,000 private schools. Department programs also provide grant, loan, and work-study assistance to more than 15 million postsecondary students.[98]

The secretary of the Department of Education could learn a thing or two from the Secretary of Commerce responsible for coordinating the writing of the report, *A Metric America: A Decision Whose Time Has Come.* That Secretary of Commerce, Maurice Stans, submitted the report to the Congress along with the letter in Figure 7.1, setting out nine specific recommendations to be implemented in order to achieve a metric America, once and for all.

Maurice Stans's legacy is one of an enlightened and transcendental secretary of commerce. Had all his recommendations been implemented, today the United States would be number one or at least in the top ten on the PISA test. He was to trade and commerce what Henry Kissinger and James Baker were to foreign policy. Note two specific standouts on his list of recommendations: "That early priority be given to educate every American school child and the public at large to think in metric," and "That the Congress, after deciding on a plan for the nation, establish a target date ten years ahead, by which time the U.S. will have become predominantly, though not exclusively metric."

The phrase, "though not exclusively metric" shows pragmatism. It says that we shouldn't expect that every last element of American life should be metric. For example, sports that are characteristically American should not be expected to change in their use of USCS units. The baseball diamond would still consist of bases 90 feet apart, and football would continue to use the down system of 10 yards per down. Indeed, there is a place for USCS units, but in order for our K–12 students to benefit, particularly in the beginning grades, we must be predominantly metric not only in the curriculum but in the culture at large for cognitive support. Changes in weather reports, speed limits, distances, weights, and all liquid measures can be easily and constructively phased in over a ten-year period.

SIRS:

I have the honor to transmit to you the Report on the U.S. Metric Study, which was conducted by the National Bureau of Standards of the Department of Commerce.

Thousands of individuals, firms and organized groups, representative of our society, participated in the Study. After weighing the extensive evidence presented by these participants, this report concludes that the United States should change to the metric system through a coordinated national program.

I agree with this conclusion, and therefore recommend

— That the United States change to the International Metric System deliberately and carefully;
— That this be done through a coordinated national program;
— That the Congress assign the responsibility for guiding the change, and anticipating the kinds of special problems described in the report, to a central coordinating body responsive to all sectors of our society;
— That within this guiding framework, detailed plans and timetables be worked out by these sectors themselves;
— That early priority be given to educating every American schoolchild and the public at large to think in metric terms;
— That immediate steps be taken by the Congress to foster U.S. participation in international standards activities;
— That in order to encourage efficiency and minimize the overall costs to society, the general rule should be that any changeover costs shall "lie where they fall";
— That the Congress, after deciding on a plan for the nation, establish a target date ten years ahead, by which time the U.S. will have become predominantly, though not exclusively, metric;
— That there be a firm government commitment to this goal.

The Department of Commerce stands ready to provide whatever further assistance the Congress may require in working out a national plan and putting it into effect.

Respectfully submitted,

Maurice H. Stans
Secretary of Commerce

Figure 7.1: *Source: http://nvlpubs.nist.gov/nistpubs/sp958-lide/234-236.pdf*

Change is possible if we have the political fortitude to be persistent. It is instructive to note that after the Metric Board was disbanded, there were American politicians who were undaunted and continued to insist that the metric system is good for America. As a result, in 1988 Congressman Rostenkowski of Illinois introduced the Omnibus Trade and Competitiveness Act of 1988.[99] This bill was an amendment to the Metric Act of 1975. The problem was that its primary thrust was still to facilitate international trade and commerce. The value-added assets of the system change that affect the education of our children, and that were mentioned in Maurice Stans's letter to the Congress have not been realized. All that has been achieved so far amounts to no more than tinkering at the edges of total change. Thus, we continue to suffer the consequences, particularly in mathematics and science education.

In the last campaign for president of the United States, some candidates argued for abolishment of the ED. When we compare the proposal of the Commerce Department in the time of Maurice Stans to the current signature proposal of ED's Secretary Arne Duncan, the Common Core State Standards, the case is convincingly made that maybe the department should indeed be abolished. Whereas the Commerce Department in the 1960s proposed to educate children in metric, the current ED here in the twenty-first century is proposing cutting back on the public school system, in the interest of creating more privately managed charter schools. Had the recommendations of the Commerce Department of the 1960s been fully implemented, American students would not have placed thirtieth in the world on the PISA test in 2012, and, in my opinion, we would not need a Department of Education.

There must be a demonstrative raison d'être for the Education Department of our country, or else it becomes a bureaucratic extension that engages in wasteful spending of taxpayers' money on spurious initiatives to justify its existence. When the 2009 PISA results (where the US placed twenty-fifth in the world) were announced, an enlightened secretary of education would have asked a simple question: is there a common element, in the mathematics and science curriculum, in all of the countries whose students outperform students in the US? A check of the related elementary school curriculum in all these countries, including our northern neighbor Canada, would have shown that they all utilize the metric system of measurements and that all their students **think in metric**. Had Secretary Duncan done this, combined with analysis of the history of attempts to change measurements systems in this country, he would have had a more productive tenure to justify the existence of his office. He could then have advised President Obama that the only reason we continue to use the USCS in our curriculum is because of the error of not requiring a change to the metric system. He could have further advocated for a phasing-in methodology, as recommended by the US Commerce Department. He would have gleaned from historical analysis that one of the reasons the US is not a metric system country today is because of the decision to ignore the suggestion for a mandatory change, through a carefully planned phasing-in period of ten years.

As we look to the future, it is clear that we must change to the metric system if we are to address the low student performances in science and mathematics. Let's consider, for example, the change from the Fahrenheit scale to the Celsius scale. This is another case where an enlightened secretary of education could act. He could have enlisted the Federal Communication Commission (FCC) to draft new regulations stipulating that all television and radio broadcasts must begin to phase in the Celsius scale, by stating temperatures in both Fahrenheit and Celsius. In cable television broadcasts, *BBC World News* (*BBCWN*) does exactly that. All weather reports and forecasts give temperatures in both Celsius and Fahrenheit. If all cable television and radio networks started this practice, this would begin the public education process. Radio and television stations give temperature readings at various times of the day, seven days per week. On television, it is particularly visual, and psychologically effective, with five-day forecasts projecting the daily high and low temperatures. Young American minds would absorb the Celsius patterns as a sponge would absorb a liquid. Americans would be receptive and appreciative of the phasing-in process, and at the end of ten years, a seamless transition from the USCS to the MS would be accomplished.

Acquaintance with the Fahrenheit scale has conditioned most Americans to be psychologically locked into the number ranges that inform us when and how to dress appropriately for daily routines and other activities throughout the year. This is because we are thinking in USCS units. A gradual transition over ten years would cause minimal inconvenience for Americans, while giving our students the tools they need for mathematics and science. Before you know it, the United States would join its international counterparts, and, with the money we spend per student, our education system would be the best in the world.

Since we live in a representative republic, we must be prepared to counter myopic and cynical politicians and agenda-driven groups who could frame the suggested change as "un-American," in language that exacerbates the resistance to change. The current Education Department and its secretary can be forceful advocates for change with a strategy to counter powerful interest groups such as Americans for Customary Weight and Measures (ACWM). This group had significant influence in the rejection of the metric system in the past. Its chairman, Seaver Leslie, described this rejection as "celebrating the poetry, practicality and accuracy" of our "superior English units."[100] He conveniently did not mention, or perhaps he was unaware, that Great Britain, the country of origin of the "English units," abandoned that system in 1965. He also was ignorant of the fact that George Washington implored the Congress to make the change to metric in 1790. In the current age, where the electronic chip technology is supreme, scientific measurements are characterized by use of the meter and its decimalized sub-units. For example, in nanotechnology, the nanometer (one billionth of a meter) is mathematically expressed as 10^{-9} meter. I would challenge Seaver Leslie to give a similarly elegant, poetic, and accurate and standardized representation using non-decimal USCS units such as the inch, the foot or the yard.

The change to metric will inevitably incur some cost, as most investments do. But an investment must be considered in terms of the potential for profit and dividend. The problem is that investments are currently being made with taxpayers' money, but they are doomed for a precipitous loss. It will be shown in the next chapter that over $5 billion was given to the Education Department during the financial collapse of 2008, and that a significant part of that money was spent on implementing the Common Core State Standards, a move that was spearheaded by Education Secretary Arne Duncan. One is tempted to ask, what would be the result if that money had been spent on defraying some of the cost of changing measurements systems? What if states were offered federal grants from that $5 billon to update mathematics textbooks and curricula to support the change to metric? What if some of that money were spent to defray the cost of creating speed limits road signs in both KPH and MPH for ten years and to subsidize gas stations to display price per liter together with price per gallon?

As for the ordinary American citizen, had the Commerce Department's recommendations been actualized, today we would be living in a metric system culture, and **thinking in metric**. The environmental impact would not only facilitate the education of children, but also Americans traveling to other countries, whether as tourists or on business. In such cases, when we see speed limits in kilometers per hour (KPH), we wouldn't have to calculate that a kilometer is equivalent to 0.6 of a mile. The mile (each of which is 5280 feet) has no significance when we learn to think in metric. We also wouldn't have to think or make calculations when temperatures are given in Celsius rather than in Fahrenheit. When we learn that the temperature is 30°C we would intuitively grasp that this is "hot" weather temperature, and would not need to ask for the equivalent in °F.

In a phasing-in process, there are creative ways to help Americans adults and children to switch from USCS to metric. Those who are psychologically locked into the current system and whose daily routines may be initially affected by the Celsius scale may need to be helped in the transition from Fahrenheit to Celsius. Regarding Celsius, the following two mnemonics can help to make the transition very effective:

> *When it's zero it's freezing,*
> *when it's 10 it's not,*
> *when it's 20 it's warm,*
> *when it's 30 it's hot!*

Or, stated in reverse:

> *Thirty is hot*
> *Twenty is nice*
> *Ten is cool*
> *Zero is ice*

Source: *http://lamar.colostate.edu/~hillger/temps.htm*

The change in television broadcast technology from **analog** to **digital** is instructive because it was a relatively smooth changeover, without any significant disruptions. The key to the success of that change process was the well-planned phasing-in period. The Federal Communications Commission (FCC) set the change in progress in 1996, and through the process set the final date for complete digital broadcast for June 12, 2009.[101]

As we may recall from chapter 1, Jamaica was grouped with the US in a CIA report as one of only of three countries still using the Fahrenheit scale. The point was also made that even though action was late in coming, Jamaica followed all other British Commonwealth countries and eventually went metric in 1998 (See figure 2.2). In that country, road signs are now in kilometers per hour (KPH). For the American tourist visiting the island and engaged in driving, this is not an issue since the modern automobile speedometer is calibrated in MPH as well as KPH. Phasing in Celsius in media outlets was a seamless process through 2010. Not only did the process facilitate adult Jamaicans, but also it was accommodating to the large number of American tourists visiting the island, who have been conditioned to Fahrenheit. Now, temperatures are expressed only in Celsius in most media outlets.

As for the pure metric measurements, I recently visited Jamaica and ordered a Red Stripe lager beer while at dinner. I observed that the bottom of the bottle stated the liquid measure in milliliters as 341 mL. See Photograph 1.

On my return to the US, I bought the same brand of lager beer in a similar size bottle, and the liquid measure stated at the bottom was in USCS units as fluid ounces or "11.2 Fl oz." See Photograph 2.

This brings up another confusion in the USCS measurements. How many elementary school children in this country know the difference between a **fluid ounce** and a **regular (avoirdupois) ounce**? Then there is a third kind in this category called the **troy ounce**. Troy ounces are used mostly for measuring metals such as gold or silver. Not only do words like feet and yards bear no visual similarity (as milliliters and liters do), but unrelated concepts like the three types of ounce look related because of their names. There is very little commercial and certainly no educational necessity for these kinds of measures.

Photograph 1: *Red Stripe Lager Beer bought in Jamaica (Dillon Lobban)*   **Photograph 2**: *Red Stripe Lager Beer bought in the United States (Dillon Lobban)*

The above demonstrations shows that Jamaica, which entered the metric system in 1998, now has its people—adults and children—**thinking in metric**, while this great industrial giant, the United States of America, has Americans and students still pondering USCS units such as fluid ounces vs. avoirdupois ounces. If Jamaica becomes an OEOC country and participates in the PISA test, it may well place ahead of the US, as happened when Jamaica placed higher than the US in the 1998 spelling bee contest.[102] In the 2012 PISA test, as we may recall, the US was nowhere to be seen in mathematics in the top twenty-nine countries. It is hard to understand why American leaders don't seem to even consider the likeliest culprit, i.e., the persistence and ubiquity of the USCS.

Transformative educational leadership is needed in the United States. The leadership of Secretary of Education Arne Duncan fell far short of an enlightened educational leader. He must take responsibility for the consequences of his actions, particularly with the implementation of Common Core.

Of course, it would be palpably unfair to assign complete culpability to Arne Duncan for the trending down in PISA test scores, because he did inherit the effects of past congressional inaction. In addition, he must be given some credit for the STEM program, limited in scope though it may be. But judgment of the strategies he espoused to correct the PISA problem is fair game. As will be demonstrated in chapters 8 and 9, if the Common Core is his answer to the problem, then it's time to abolish the Department of Education and consolidate its useful functions with some other department. Instead of reuniting with Health and Human Services, I would recommend that it be amalgamated with the Department of Commerce, which is on record as advocating that American children be acculturated to the metric system.

In chapter 2 through chapter 6, the argument in support of the facilitating features of the metric system and the regressive characteristics of the USCS were presented. In this chapter we discussed the fact that although there is recognition, beginning with our first president, George Washington, that having the metric system was in the best interest of the United States, we are still living and thinking in the dark ages of the USCS. We have shown that the lack of fortitude to initiate a mandatory, planned phasing-in process is the reason we are not a metric system country today, and the reason our children are doing poorly in mathematics and science.

In Part II, i.e., the next two chapters, we will dig deeper into how the Common Core States Standards (CCSS) came into being in over forty-five states. Not only will the inadequacies of the CCSS be discussed, but it will be shown that its hasty rollout was motivated by a desire to exploit available federal funds.

PART II

WHAT'S WRONG
WITH COMMON CORE

CHAPTER 8:
The Controversial Nature of the Common Core State Standards

Previous chapters gave cause-and-effect information regarding the persistent trending down in PISA mathematics scores of American students from 2000 through 2012. With this state of affairs in the background of American education, and with politicians blaming teacher quality for the low performance outcomes, the emergence of the Common Core State Standards (CCSS) as an educational remedy takes on added significance. However, in retrospect, it is difficult to find any educational reform initiative in the last fifty years that has galvanized opposition by parents, teachers, educational professionals, school principals, and school communities at large as much as the CCSS. Writing about the circumstance and time of arrival of the CCSS, Dianne Ravitch, education research professor at New York University since 1995 and prolific writer on American education policy issues, said it best:

They [the CCSS] arrive at a time when American public education and its teachers are under attack. Never have public schools been as subject to upheaval, assault, and chaos as they are today. Unlike modern corporations, which extol creative disruption, schools need stability, not constant turnover and change. Yet for the past dozen years, ill-advised federal and state policies have rained down on students, teachers, principals, and schools.[103]

The CCSS was written with the hope of getting unfettered support, not only by politicians but also by the educational community at large. Instead, there is widespread opposition and overt dissatisfaction. The following statement reflecting teacher opposition was reported on *politico.com*:

The board of the New York state teachers union this weekend unanimously withdrew its support for the Common Core standards as they have been implemented—a major blow for Common Core advocates who have been touting support from teachers as proof that the standards will succeed in classrooms nationwide.[104]

Then there was the report from NBC Washington:

An Iowa woman jokingly calls it "Satan's handiwork." A California mom says she's broken down in tears. A Pennsylvania parent says it "makes my blood boil." What could be so horrible? Grade-school math. As schools around the U.S. implement national Common Core learning standards, parents trying to help their kids with math homework say that adding, subtracting, multiplying and dividing has become as complicated as calculus.[105]

According to the *Washington Post*, three states viewed the name "Common Core" pejoratively, and as such have taken steps to rename the program:

*Arizona Gov. Jan Brewer (R) used an executive order to strip
the name "Common Core" from the state's new math and
reading standards for public schools. In the Hawkeye State,
the same standards are now called "The Iowa Core." And
in Florida, lawmakers want to delete "Common Core" from
official documents and replace it with the cheerier-sounding
"Next Generation Sunshine State Standards."[106]*

The remainder of this chapter will be centered on answering the
following questions. Why are the Common Core State Standards so
controversial? What was their underlying purpose? How were they
constructed and implemented, and why? Who are the personalities
involved, and what are their motives? How do the Common Core
Standards compare with other educational reform initiatives?

8.1 A Hasty Rollout and the Charter Schools Imperative

After reading the article "Everything You Need to Know about
Common Core" by Dianne Ravitch, and knowing that she was assistant
secretary of education under two presidents of opposing parties,
George H. W. Bush and Bill Clinton, I've made the judgment that no
one is more qualified to discuss policy issues affecting the character of
the CCSS. My judgment was bolstered by the following excerpt from
her curriculum vitae:

*From 1997 to 2004, she was a member of the National
Assessment Governing Board, which oversees the National
Assessment of Educational Progress, the federal testing
program. She was appointed by the Clinton administration's
Secretary of Education Richard Riley in 1997 and
reappointed by him in 2001. From 1995 until 2005, she
held the Brown Chair in Education Studies at the Brookings
Institution and edited* Brookings Papers on Education
Policy. *Before entering government service, she was Adjunct
Professor of History and Education at Teachers College,
Columbia University.[107]*

The article mentioned above was a presentation given by Ravitch at a meeting of the Modern Language Association (MLA). It was given after meetings with David Coleman, the acknowledged architect of the CCSS. The following statement describes the hasty construction and rollout dynamics of the standards:

> *The Common Core standards were developed in 2009 and released in 2010. Within a matter of months, they had been endorsed by 45 states and the District of Columbia. At present, publishers are aligning their materials with the Common Core, technology companies are creating software and curriculum aligned with the Common Core, and two federally-funded consortia have created online tests of the Common Core.*[108]

That hasty rollout of the Common Core in 2010 prompts the question: What was behind the urgency? Was it to address an existing educational problem such as the poor mathematics/science performance of American students on the 2009 PISA test? As stated before, in 2009 the United States placed twenty-fifth in mathematics and twenty-fourth in science among sixty-four countries.[109]

It turns out that $5 billion in federal funding was made available to states by Secretary of Education Arne Duncan to implement educational reform, under the umbrella of the "Race to the Top" program. According to Diane Ravitch:

> *In response to the economic crisis of 2008, Congress gave the U.S. Department of Education $5 billion to promote "reform." Secretary Duncan launched a competition for states called "Race to the Top."*[110]

The conditions for receiving funding from that money were laid out by the education secretary, as follows:

> *If states wanted any part of that money, they had to agree to certain conditions. They had to agree to evaluate teachers*

to a significant degree by the rise or fall of their students'
test scores; **they had to agree to increase the number**
of privately managed charter schools; *they had to*
agree to adopt "college and career ready standards," which
were understood to be the not-yet-finished Common Core
standards.[111]

To put it succinctly, states were required, by the secretary of education, to use student performance on tests created by an unfinished educational product, the "not-yet-finished" CCSS, to evaluate teachers, principals, schools, and support staff all across the nation with dire consequences, such as closing schools and firing staff if they fell short in such evaluations.

The obvious scheme was that with the closing of public schools, and wholesale firing of entire staffs in such schools, the only alternative for the education of the nation's children would be a system of privately managed charter schools. Privately managed charter schools are being run for profit, and for that reason teachers and support staff in these schools are paid substantially less than in public schools. In most charter schools, faculty and staff are offered fewer benefits and less job protection than they would in the public school system, where school districts are legally obligated to honor union contracts. One of the characteristics of many charter schools is that they are allowed to be very selective of the students they admit. The following statement about the selective process is a case in point:

> *Reuters has found that across the United States, charters*
> *aggressively screen student applicants, assessing their*
> *academic records, parental support, disciplinary history,*
> *motivation, special needs and even their citizenship,*
> *sometimes in violation of state and federal law.*[112]

This meticulous selection of higher performing students enables charter schools to present themselves as exceptional schools, when in fact, their successes are largely due to admitting only highly motivated students with better-than-average academic records. By law, regular public schools cannot be selective, and therefore have no choice but to admit and educate all students, including those who are middle and lower performing, those who have inadequate prerequisite knowledge, and also students with special needs.

Pushing a reform product that was "not yet finished," and therefore was neither piloted nor field-tested for efficacy, then using that product to evaluate teachers is not only crassly unfair but palpably destructive of our system of education. In using federal funding as a hook, states were prompted to be receptive of the CCSS, and so, "Race to the Top" became a race to get federal funding.

Experienced educational professionals understand that efficacy determination is the sine qua non of large curriculum-altering initiatives, particularly for nationwide implementation. On the issue of lack of field-testing for the CCSS, Diane Ravitch informed us as follows:

> *In 2009, I urged its leaders to plan on field testing them to find out how the standards worked in real classrooms with real teachers and real students. Only then would we know whether they improve college-readiness and equity.*[113]

It is reasonable to infer that in the hurry to get the program ready, so that states could get a share of the $5 billion in the "Race to the Top," funding took priority over testing for efficacy. As anyone would expect, this obviously non-empirical approach to the education of children was not well taken by professional educators. Here again is education historian Diane Ravitch:

> *When it became clear that there would be no field testing, I decided I could not support the standards. I objected to the lack of any democratic participation in their development; I objected to the absence of any process for revising them, and I was fearful that they were setting unreachable targets for most students.*[114]

Award-winning New York school principal Carol Burris concurred when she wrote:

- 130 -

Part of the problem with the rushed implementation of this reform is that there was never sufficient opportunity for schools to carefully examine and critique the standards themselves. In the field, it has been "whack a mole" as districts implement evaluation systems, testing and data driven networks while wading through thousands of pages of modules.[115]

Now the standards are in full implementation across the nation. The contracted publishers, software developers, and at least two federally funded consortia have raked in their share of federal largesse, but what are the results so far?

Here is Ravitch's perception:

My fears were confirmed by the Common Core. Wherever they have been implemented, they have caused a dramatic collapse of test scores. In state after state, the passing rates dropped by about 30%. This was not happenstance. This was failure by design.[116]

"Failure by design" is a serious indictment of a program that, as we will later learn, was presented as a "once-in-a-generation opportunity" by its architect, David Coleman, about whom more will be said later. "Failure by design" suggests that there is a specific objective, with built-in strategies to ensure that failure occurs. But who would be the beneficiaries of failure by design? One of the key features of CCSS is teacher and school evaluations based on test scores. The tests were created by a publishing company, and so teachers had no control over content or structure. If test scores were low, teachers, schools and support staff would be cited for incompetence, principals would be fired and public schools would be closed. Here again the school principal Carol Burris:

It is easy to point fingers at the teacher or school for giving the test, or to point fingers at Pearson for creating it. The problem, however, goes much deeper. The problem (no pun intended) is at the core.[117]

8.2 Personalities of the Common Core State Standards

The term "Common Core" and the name "David Coleman" have become synonymous. The previously mentioned presentation by Diane Ravitch at the MLA conference was originally scheduled and mutually agreed upon as a joint presentation with David Coleman, since he "is generally acknowledged as the architect of the Common Core Standards."[118] Unfortunately, Coleman was conspicuously absent from the presentation. According to Diane Ravitch, had he been present, "he would not be able to explain why so many educators and parents are now opposed to the standards and are reacting angrily to the testing that accompanies them."[119]

But who is David Coleman? It turns out that on the one hand he is a man of impressive academic credentials. Graduating with a BA in philosophy at Yale, he studied literature at Oxford University as a Rhodes Scholar and went on to specialize in philosophy at Cambridge University. On the other hand, I could find no evidence that he has content or pedagogical knowledge in mathematics or in science education. I could also find no record that Coleman had any experience as a K–12 teacher, school administrator, curriculum specialist, or writer of educational standards.

David Coleman is one of three cofounders of an organization called "Student Achievement Partners (SAP)." The second was Jason Zimba, professor of mathematics and physics employed at Bennington College, where by an interesting coincidence, David Coleman's mother, Elizabeth Coleman, was president. Zimba was a fellow Rhodes Scholar with Coleman at Oxford. The third cofounder is Susan Pimentel, who is a lawyer with a bachelor of science (BS) degree in early-childhood education. In effect, the CCSS is a product of SAP, since the three cofounders were the lead writers of the program.

Here's an excerpt from the purpose statement of SAP, as it relates to the CCSS:

> *As educators, as researchers, and as citizens, we view the changes brought by the college and career readiness focus on*

the Common Core State Standards as a once-in-a-generation opportunity for kids of all backgrounds and ability levels to better fulfill their potential.[120]

When I read this, I was reminded of a catchphrase question posed in the 1980s by a Wendy's commercial, which was used by presidential candidate Walter Mondale against Gary Hart. That question was, "Where's the beef?"[121]

Two things jumped out at me in the purpose statement. The first was the acknowledgement that this "once-in-a-generation opportunity" was merely a point of view of the SAP. Having a "view" does not affirm educational efficacy for a program to be implemented nationwide targeting millions of school children. Efficacy can only come from data collected through empirical methodologies such as field testing or piloting. The second thing that hit me, minor though it may be, was the casual use of the word "kids," in a formal educational reform document. From my perspective, any solidly grounded authentic educational professional would have used the word "students." I can't imagine young women or young men in the twelfth grade at ages sixteen or seventeen being referred to as "kids."

Be that as it may, the naively constructed product of SAP was bought, hook, line, and sinker, by Secretary of Education Arne Duncan despite the not-yet-finished status of David Coleman's educational reform product.

The societal and public school pushback has been enormous. Instead of recognizing the error of his ways in accepting and supporting the CCSS, Arne Duncan was most unkind in his remarks about parents. In an address to the Council of Chief State School Officers organization, here is Duncan in his own words:

It's fascinating to me that some of the pushback is coming from, sort of, white suburban moms who—all of a sudden— their child isn't as brilliant as they thought they were and their school isn't as good as they thought they were, and that's pretty scary.[122]

Here we have a secretary of education of the United States resorting to invectives directed at parents rather than elucidating the merits of the CCSS by stating its positive aspects from his perspective — or better still, from data. His behavior reflects the fact that he had no substantive perspective and that his support of the CCSS had no basis, because he accepted it before it was finished and before he had any empirical basis for its national implementation.

Such is the history of education reform. A small group or a person with impressive transcript-based academic credentials ponder an educational idea and couch it in conjectural language that offers plausible-sounding premises as to the feasibility of the idea. The next step is to find funding sources and political support. In the case where federal funding is available, the first requirement is to write a proposal. If the proposal has the right language and is presented to the right people, the program specified in the proposal is accepted and implemented without being piloted or field-tested. Later, when the outcomes prove to be ineffective at best and harmful at worst, the initiative is terminated or transitioned into oblivion, most times without accountability. The usual consequence is that we end up losing whole generations of students while wasting taxpayers' money to the tune of billions of dollars.

Not only do the Common Core State Standards fall into that process category, but there are two consequential negative implications. First, most of the other ineffective and now defunct programs were localized to states or particular school districts, whereas the CCSS has metastasized to over forty-five states. All indications point to its nationwide ineffectiveness as a tool for comprehensive reform in mathematics education. Second, the states' acceptance of the CCSS has a primary, explicit, and disturbing goal: that the untested reform product should be used as a tool for the evaluation of teachers, principals, and schools through test scores with the intent of creating more privately managed charter schools at the expense of the public school system. In effect, the CCSS was accepted not to improve, but to radically modify and ultimately destroy the public school system, nationwide.

Diane Ravitch has laid out the draconian requirements to which states had to conform:

*They had to agree to "turnaround" low-performing schools
by such tactics as firing the principal and part or all of the
school staff; and they had to agree to collect unprecedented
amounts of personally identifiable information about every
student and store it in a data warehouse.*[123]

We have looked at the evolution of the CCSS as an unempirical architectural product of David Coleman's SAP. We have made the point that states had to commit to firing of teachers and closing schools as well as to creating more privately managed charter schools in order to receive funding for an unfinished educational product. But there is another dimension to the story of the CCSS, and it is as blatantly political as it is profoundly disturbing.

8.3 Michelle Rhee and David Coleman

We may recall activist educational administrator Michelle Rhee, the so-called "Educational Heavyweight," former chancellor of the Washington, DC, schools, and the controversy surrounding her stormy relations with principals and staff in that school system. It turns out that she was intricately associated with the CCSS architect and SAP cofounder David Coleman. Before getting to the Rhee-Coleman relationship, let's get a number of perspectives on the real Michelle Rhee.

In an article entitled the "The Disturbing Connection between David Coleman and Michelle Rhee," Diane Ravitch wrote:

*Rhee is a lightning rod. She has advocated for policies
that will remove all job protections from teachers. She has
supported rightwing governors who want to destroy teacher
unions. She advocates for charters and vouchers. She has
accepted millions of dollars from known and unknown
sources to promote privatization. She has spent millions of
dollars to support candidates—usually from the far right—who
agree with her views. She treats test scores as the sine qua
non of education. She is a darling of the far right.*[124]

On the job as chancellor of the Washington School System, Rhee is regarded by many of her former teachers and principals as lacking in basic administrative skills, particularly in the human-relations domain. According to the Washington Post, Rachel Levy, who is a graduate of the DC school system and who later became a social studies teacher in the same schools, wrote the following:

> Rhee's ideas about how to fix the ailing school system were largely misinformed, and it's no wonder: She knew little about instruction, curriculum, management, fiscal matters, and community relations. She was, to be sure, abrasive...But as education historian Diane Ravitch has said, "It's difficult to win a war when you're firing on your own troops."[125]

After stepping down as chancellor of the Washington School System, Michelle Rhee formed her own educational organization called "Student First." Here is a description of Rhee's organization, found in *The New Republic*:

> Student First, Rhee's post-Washington organization, lobbies state legislatures around the country to pass education-reform measures. Although it began in a series of meetings in Washington among the influential friends Rhee had made as chancellor—the names she drops in telling of its founding include Rahm Emanuel, Eli Broad, the Aspen Institute, the Hoover Institution, and McKinsey, and her initial requests for philanthropic funding are at the $100 million level.[126]

It is palpably clear that Michelle Rhee's multimillion-dollar enterprise, Student First, was designed with political ideological intent, rather than for the noble cause of promoting effective quality education of students. Rachelle Baye's article "The Schoolyard Fight" contains a subsection entitled, "Michelle Rhee's new organization is giving millions to support conservative candidates in dozens of states."[127]

According to Baye:

*Students First — created by former Washington, D.C. schools
chief Michelle Rhee — is leading a new wave of "education
reform" organizations, funded largely by wealthy donors,
that are challenging teachers' unions and supporting mostly
conservative candidates up and down the ticket in dozens
of states. These groups promote charter schools, voucher
programs, and weakening of employment safeguards like
teacher tenure, all ideas bitterly opposed by unions.*[128]

A number of entrepreneurs and investors looking for the next big
money-making opportunity and right-wing politicians who have an
unhealthy bias about education have expressed approval of Michelle
Rhee and her tactics, and some actually, as the saying goes, put their
money where their mouths were. According to the *Washington Post*:

*Michelle Rhee did get a lot of people to pay attention
to public education. Who? Many of them are unelected
billionaires and conservative ideologues without any
education expertise who have donated vast amounts of
money to programs that have no basis in research. Some seek
to privatize the public school system.*[129]

So what does Michelle Rhee have to with the CCSS? It turns out
that David Coleman, the Common Core architect, founder of Student
Achievement Partners, and his two lead writers of the CCSS were
employees of Michelle Rhee's Student First organization. According
to Diane Ravitch, in the previously mentioned article, regarding the
Rhee-Coleman connection:

*I learned from Ken Libby—a graduate student at the
University of Colorado who likes to read IRS filings by
advocacy organizations—that Rhee's Students First has a
board of directors; that David Coleman is the treasurer of
her board of directors; and that the other two members of
her board are employees of David Coleman's organization
Student Achievement Partners (one of the two wrote the new*

CC math standards). To those who ask Coleman why he is on Rhee's board, he responds that his term ends in June. That is non-responsive.[130]

As treasurer of Student First, David Coleman was responsible for collecting the millions of dollars from contributors to the organization, and the subsequent distribution of those funds to agenda-driven right-wing politicians. The Venn diagram in figure8.1 shows elements of the symbiotic relationship between Michelle Rhee's Student First organization and David Coleman's Student Achievement Partners. The diagram shows the collection and distribution of funds for political purposes as well as the unfair teacher evaluation standards at the intersection of both organizations.

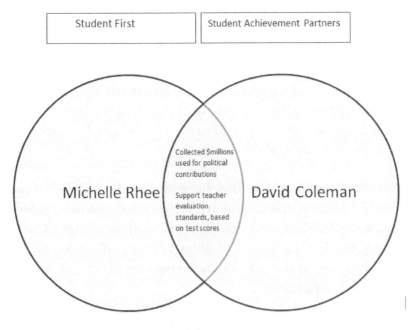

Figure 8.1

The latest news on Michelle Rhee is that she has stepped down as the leader of her "Student First" organization to accept employment with the Scotts Miracle-Grow Company in Ohio.[131] According to the *Washington Post*, Rhee now goes by the name Michelle Johnson in her new job. She is married to Sacramento mayor Kevin Johnson. The article also stated that "she was recently named interim board chairwoman of St. Hope Schools, a small group of Sacramento charter schools founded by her husband."[132]

As for David Coleman, this designer of the program he called a "once-in-a-generation opportunity," this former treasurer of Michelle Rhee's politically oriented "Student First" lobbying program has tactically meandered himself to become the current president of the College Board. According to the *New York Times*, "David Coleman, an architect of the common core curriculum standards that are being adopted in nearly all 50 states, will become the president of the College Board, starting in October."[133] The article went on to state that "Mr. Coleman will earn a base [salary] of $550,000, with total compensation of nearly $750,000.[134]

Not surprisingly, politicians could hardly wait to endorse the appointment. According to the *New York Times*: "Many other leading education figures, including Arne Duncan, the secretary of education, and former Gov. Jeb Bush of Florida also endorsed the appointment."[135]

Backed by his political support structure, will College Board President David Coleman's educational architectural skills extend to redesigning the SATs to fit the Common Core Standards? At the time of writing this letter, published reports indicate that the answer to this question is in the affirmative. Will the new SAT design be field-tested before implementation? If David Coleman's modus operandi is consistent, there will be no field-testing, as was the case with the CCSS. It will be just be another of Coleman's arbitrary unempirical implementations amounting to no more than his "view." If this modification is actualized, it would not be surprising if universities reevaluate their traditional reliance on SAT scores as a prime measure of students' precollege capabilities.

In the meantime, the CCSS is now the way of life in school districts across the nation. Teachers, parents, and children are bearing the brunt of the impositions of this insidious educational reform product, because they have little or no choice when policy initiatives are implemented in their schools.

8.4 The Junkyard of Educational Reform

Implementing educational programs without field-testing or empirical data is one of the reasons for the myriads of education reform programs that do not work in this country. The junkyard of educational reform is overflowing with all kinds of programs that had to be abandoned because they proved to be empirically ineffective.

From the 1960s to the early 1970s, for example, the concept of Individually Guided Education (IGE) swept across the nation. According to William Wiersma, writing in *ERIC*, "It is one of the few innovations that was scheduled for national implementation."[136] The program had seven major components and was rooted in educational psychology through behaviorist approaches to the learning process. In a study entitled "The Rise and Fall of Individually Guided Education," it was determined that the reasons for the demise of IGE were the unanticipated anomalies encountered over the implementation period.[137] In, short, IGE was not properly field-tested and had no empirical substantiation before implementation. History has shown that without field-testing or piloting for identification of anomalies before nationwide implementation of comprehensive programs with the scope and magnitude of IGE or the CCSS, the probability of their ending up in the educational reform junkyard is very high.

In New York State, where I worked as mathematics teacher and supervisor of a mathematics department in a high school, the three-year curriculum for the Mathematics Regents Examinations was structurally changed four times. The original curriculum consisting of algebra for the ninth grade, geometry for the tenth grade, intermediate algebra and trigonometry for the eleventh grade was changed to three respective courses of integrated mathematics. Lots of money was spent on teacher workshops over three summers. No sooner than teachers became fluent with the three-year integrated mathematics curriculum, the program was changed, by an incoming New York education commissioner, to two one-and-a-half-year course sequences called Mathematics A and Mathematics B. The changes required the same spending on teacher workshops, over several summer sessions, to facilitate transition to the new curriculum. Then guess what? A new commissioner of education decided to change again, but this time the change went back to the original three-year sequence. There was one consistent trend. As soon as New York State high school mathematics teachers got fluent in one curriculum change, they had to retool for another arbitrary change, and this went on for more than two decades.

Then in 2011, the *New York Times* published a retrospective on the status of mathematics in New York State, entitled "10 Years of Assessing Students with Scientific Exactitude." In this article, the look back included the following statement:

> **JUNE 2003:** *Scores on the state algebra test are so poorly calibrated that 70 percent of seniors fail. After a statewide outcry, officials agree to throw out the results. The Princeton Review says that ranking New York first was a mistake. "We're going to have to come up with a fiasco index for a state like New York that messes up a lot of people's lives," a spokesman says.*[138]

This is what resulted after all those curriculum changes. At the time of each change, New Yorkers were assured that the new program was the definitive solution. In the meantime, teachers and instructors were paid handsomely for those summer workshops, in order to be ready for the intricacies of the new curriculum. I too, having to attend summer workshops, was a recipient of summer workshop money. In the meantime, the sequences and magnitude of the changes created a windfall of profits for textbook companies, while taxpayers were taken to the cleaners. I have heard the cynical view that the changes were motivated not so much by a desire for educational improvements but by a desire for huge kickbacks by textbook publishers. I hasten to state that I have no verification as to the credibility of such imputation, but I can understand how parents' and teachers' frustrations can lead to that kind of thinking.

In 2011, New York State appointed a new state education commissioner. His name is Dr. John B. King Jr., and he once worked with Secretary of Education Arne Duncan, in an advisory role. Dr. King became the principal advocate of the CCSS, not only in New York but around the country. And so, the New York State Regents curriculum got another change, but according to the dictates of Common Core. Once again we were told by the New York education commissioner that this was the definitive solution. Once again we could be sure about one thing: that textbook and software companies had been raking in lots of taxpayer money and will continue to do so by providing newly required CCSS material. Paperback workbooks, for example, which are issued by individual students, can only be used once, since students are required to do their work in the workbooks. New workbooks must be printed each year for every single student, at taxpayer expense. How would you like to be the publisher with such a lucrative contract?

The sad part about all these untested programs being implemented by the wrong people for the wrong reasons is the continual wasting of billions and billions of taxpayer money over the years. In the world of education, there is a dearth of reflection, and so the waste continues from one program to the next. The previously mentioned 2003 New York algebra result is one of several cases in point, and the 2012 PISA test result in mathematics, where the United States placed thirtieth in the world, is another. As we move from generation to generation of students being educationally shortchanged, no one ever seems to be perturbed enough to demand education reform that really works. Education of US children seems to continue from one untested idea to the next. Is it any wonder that we continue to spend more money per student than any other country in the world with diminishing results to show for it?

The junkyard of educational reform is an open pit, ready to accommodate the next new "definitive solution." Will the CCSS be the next item to be carted to this junkyard? Had the so-called "definitive solutions" or proposed programs employed some aspect of scientific exactitude before implementation, we may have been able to give our students an education that is commensurate with the money we continue to spend.

The next chapter will provide more details about Dr. John B. King Jr., who resigned under public protest against Common Core. He did so while serving as New York State education commissioner and nationwide CCSS advocate, but is now US secretary of education.

We'll discuss his charter school and Common Core umbilical cord relationship with DE secretary Arne Duncan. We will also take a close look at the CCSS mathematics program from the perspective of the National Council of Teachers of Mathematics (NTCM), as well as a surprising admission by the lead mathematics writer for the CCSS.

Chapter 9:
The Common Core Standards in New York State and Beyond

In the previous chapter, we laid out elements of the nature the Common Core State Standards (CCSS) and the controversy surrounding their hasty rollout in several states. We also conjectured that it is only a matter of time before the CCSS is relegated to the education-reform junkyard. In this chapter, we'll focus on the ramifications of implementing the CCSS in New York, because the Common Core model in this state is similar to how it has been implemented across the country. We will explore the spurious nature of the charter school creation imperative and especially its link to CCSS teacher-evaluation components based on test scores. We will also delineate, from the perspective of the National Council of Teachers of Mathematics (NCTM), the specific anomalies found in the Common Core mathematics curriculum. After all this, we'll attempt to answer the question as to where we are headed as a country, particularly on the issue of K–12 education in mathematics and science.

9.1 The Charter School Imperative and Common Core Teacher Evaluation

You may recall that one of the conditions stipulated by Secretary of Education Arne Duncan is that states must agree to "increase the number of privately managed charter schools" in order to receive their share of the $5 billion federal funding for CCSS.

Over a period of three years beginning in 2011, there were three extraordinary occurrences involving Arne Duncan and one high-ranking New York State education official. The first was in 2011, when the *New York Times* ran a report with the headline "Charter Founder Is Named Education Commissioner."[139] That commissioner was Dr. John B. King Jr., and the state was New York. The second occurrence took place three years later, in 2014, and was reported in the general media. According to the *New York Times*:

> *New York State's education commissioner, John B. King Jr., who has been a staunch advocate for the Common Core standards and a frequent target of those who criticize them, announced on Wednesday that he would step down at the end of the year to take the second-highest-ranking job at the federal Education Department, senior adviser to Secretary Arne Duncan.*[140]

Thus after an awkward and stormy tenure as the chief state school officer in New York, John B. King Jr. had a smooth transition to become senior advisor to Arne Duncan. The third incident was that Arne Duncan resigned as secretary of education and John King was rewarded for his Common Core advocacy by being appointed secretary of education. This meteoric rise to the highest office in education is the culmination of a relationship that began several years earlier.

In 2011, previous to King's elevation to education commissioner in New York, Arne Duncan appointed him to be a member of the Excellence in Education Commission in an advisory role to the secretary of education. At that time, King was deputy commissioner of education in the state. In that position he was instrumental in getting

Federal funding from Arne Duncan to implement the Common Core in New York State. According to a report by the TAC-D Summer Institute:

Before becoming Commissioner, Commissioner King served as Senior Deputy Commissioner for P–12 Education at NYSED. In that role, Commissioner King coordinated the development of New York State's successful Race to the Top application, which earned the second highest point total of the winning states in Round 2 and secured $696.6 million to support the P–12 education reform agenda of the Board of Regents.[141]

The matter of King's resignation as education commissioner prompts two questions: Why did he quit the job before his tenure was complete? What really happened to cause him to leave the job as commissioner, a position that gave him administrative control over curriculum issues in the state's public school system?

In his position, King had been a relentless supporter of the CCSS. Media reports have him going around the country defending Common Core with passion and enthusiasm. In the language of the *New York Times*, "He was a firm defender of the Common Core and the tougher tests, saying the old standards had been set too low and did not reflect the skills students needed for college or jobs."[142]

We must be reminded that when Arne Duncan announced the charter schools proclamation, the CCSS with all its curriculum modifications and teacher evaluation components was not yet finished. Hence it is not unreasonable to suspect that the motive for the application for federal funding had more to do with creating more private charter schools, through a deliberate "failure by design" system, than for any known value-added asset the CCSS would bring to mathematics education in New York.

This prompts another question. Apart from being a charter school entrepreneur, what qualified John B. King Jr. to be commissioner of education of a large state such as New York? Here is a part of his curriculum vitae (CV):

Commissioner King earned a B.A. in Government from Harvard University, an M.A. in the Teaching of Social Studies from Teachers College, Columbia University, a J.D. from Yale Law School, and an Ed.D. in Educational Administrative Practice from Teachers College, Columbia University.[143]

Like David Coleman, the Common Core architect, John B. King Jr. has an impressive list of transcript-based academic credentials. Also like David Coleman, there is no record that he has any background in mathematics education. And yet they both advocate that mathematics test scores of an untested and unpiloted curriculum be used to evaluate teachers and schools, to the point where jobs would be lost and public schools will be closed, with privately managed charter schools ready to pick up the remnants. It is worth noting that privately managed charter schools pay teachers less and offer fewer benefits than the public school system, and teacher unions are not welcome.

Other than transcript-based credentials, what overarching educational experience does John B. King Jr. possess to become Commissioner of New York State? According to the *New York Times*, "Dr. King decided he wanted to become a social studies teacher, and earned his master's degree from Teachers College at Columbia University." The article went on to state that "He had no more than three years experience as a teacher, when he entered the charter school business."[144]

Dr. King is a charter school entrepreneur par excellence. He began his charter school career when he co-founded Roxbury Prep, a charter middle school in Massachusetts. He then went on to become managing director of "Uncommon Schools," a collection of charter schools in three states: New York, New Jersey, and Massachusetts.[145] Did Dr. King advise Arne Duncan to include the charter school imperative for states to get federal funding for the CCSS?

Privately managed charter schools have become big business in the crosshairs of Wall Street investors. The following excerpt is taken from an article by Jesse Stanford, in the *Huffington Post*:

Charter schools are "a favorite cause of many of the wealthy founders of New York hedge funds." The word you're probably looking for is "yippee"...
Despite the risks, charter schools are big business. Pearson, the company that sells tests and curricula to public schools, also sells tests and curricula to charter schools, and JPMorgan Chase of worldwide economic meltdown fame is bullish on charter school construction.[146]

The dilemma for John King is the perception that his primary focus, after his initial engagements with Arne Duncan, was on creating as many privately managed charter schools as possible. He has used his position as state education commissioner to implement and then enforce policies that would result in firing whole school staffs and closing schools based on CCSS test score assessments. King's unrelenting defense of the Common Core Standards would appear to have a great deal to do with the extended benefits he can eventually accrue, through the creation of more privately managed charter schools. When he vacates his job as education secretary, he will have the option of returning to his charter school entrepreneurial enterprises with an enhanced resume and a rich collection of charter schools.

King's curriculum vitae also shows that he is a lawyer. While being state education commissioner, his unrelenting advocacy for acceptance of the CCSS makes him a de facto defense attorney in the court of public opinion, with a very bright and lucrative future for himself in the charter school business.

There is an old saying that "the proof of the pudding is in the eating." In this case, the pudding is the CCSS, and New York got its taste. During King's administration, the outcries against Common Core became loud and clear. As has been reported in the New York news media, several groups of teachers and parents have combined to protest the CCSS. *CBS News* reported on two such groups protesting in Long Island, New York. Each group, such as the one in the photograph in figure 9.1, consisted of parents and teachers. In one district there were 800 protestors, and in the other there were over 1,500.

At one demonstration against Common Core, where signs demanded the resignation of John King, he was unfazed by being booed. He responded by insisting that the CCSS is a very effective set of standards. According to the report:

> *King urged the crowd to give Common Core a chance to be*
> *successful and tried to explain how student's test scores are*
> *used to weigh teachers' performance evaluations under a*
> *controversial system that became law this year.*[147]

King should have been aware of two things. First that the CCSS was not field-tested for efficacy and that rating teachers on test scores of a dubious curriculum product filled with anomalies was one of the main points of the protest. Second, he should have known that an educational reform program should not be dependent on "chance" for success, when the education of children, the jobs of educational professionals, and the future of schools are at stake. Had the CCSS been rigorously fielded-tested for efficacy, King would have been armed with a convincing set of empirical data points with which to make his case as to the viability, efficacy, and legitimacy of the CCSS. Instead, here we have an education commissioner of New York State, a former social studies teacher with only three years of experience under his belt, advocating that "chance" be the operative paradigm in a nationwide program that greatly modified the mathematics curriculum.

Promoting the untested CCSS as educationally effective, when its real purpose is the proliferation of profit-making charter schools, is opportunistic at best and deceptive at worst. The larger question, not only for New York but for the American people, is what effect will Common Core have on mathematics and science education going forward in this country? Sadly for New York State, although the education commissioner and Common Core proponent and advocate is gone, the CCSS curricula continues. More details of specific mathematics educational anomalies as experienced by one New York school will be discussed in Section 9.3. In the next section, we will expand on the negative effects of the CCSS, particularly in mathematics education.

Figure 9.1: *Parents and teachers protest against the Common Core academic standards on November 13, 2013, outside Mineola High*

(credit: Mona Rivera/1010 WINS)[148]
Source: http://newyork.cbslocal.com/2013/11/13/emotions-high-at-common-core-forum-on-long-island/

9.2 The Common Core Standards and Mathematics Education

To determine how the CCSS will affect mathematics education, not only in New York but across the country, we'll turn to the leading professional organization of K–12 mathematics educational professionals, the National Council of Teachers of Mathematics (NTCM). Its membership consists of the best teachers of mathematics in the country and has global influence in content, and even more so in mathematical pedagogy. Over twenty-five years ago, the organization issued the "Curriculum and Evaluation Standards for Teaching Mathematics" as a national guide for mathematics education.[149] These standards were updated periodically and have steered the K–12 mathematics curricula well into the twenty-first century.

Did Student Achievement Partners, who wrote the CCSS, consult with the NTCM in the construction of Common Core mathematics? There is no evidence that the NTCM was an active participant. In fact, as will be shown later, it is apparent that the writers of the CCSS had minimal or no contact with the organization.

Regarding the explicit effectiveness of the metric system for mathematics education, and the importance of its influence on learning, here is the NCTM's stated position, eloquently articulated by Henry Kepner, when he was president of the organization:

> NCTM *advocates that every student be comfortable with and proficient in use of the metric system. There can be no retreat from this position! It is our responsibility to help students become proficient in the units of measure that they will use in school, the workplace, and their neighborhoods (NCTM 2006).*[150]

As for the disadvantage of having both the MS and the USCS, as is the case with packaging and bottling here in the US, here again is the NTCM's president Kepner:

> *In the U.S., we have the distraction of living with and using both the metric and the customary (English) systems. Despite decades of efforts by NCTM, scientific societies, and many industries, along with the passage of federal laws, we encounter many commercial and social arenas where metric units are not used.*[151]

The NTCM has been a monumental resource for mathematics teachers through national and regional professional conferences and through its publications. The organization deserves to be consulted if structural changes are to be made in the mathematics education curriculum across the country. Let's peruse the NTCM's public comments on Common Core mathematics.

While giving some credit to the CCSS for being "generally consistent with the process standards in NCTM's *Principles and Standards for School Mathematics* in its strands across content areas,"[152] the NTCM was unsparing in its criticism of several aspects of the CCSS reconstruction of the K–12 mathematics curriculum. The following is the NTCM's general overview of the CCSS:

*The mathematical practices are not consistently set out as
elements of, or carefully connected with, the K–12 grade-
level and high school Standards for Understanding and
Skills. Without consistent, explicit recommendations
for the mathematical practices, it is unlikely that future
assessments, and consequently instruction, will adequately
address them.*[153]

No one can conclude that the CCSS is totally devoid of elements of some merit. Children will obviously learn some essential concepts in mathematics under the CCSS. The concern is whether or not the CCSS is optimally complete for a comprehensive precollege preparation in the subject. As regards English Language Arts (ELA), I've met teachers who conclude that CCSS has effective elements that could improve reading literacy. As to the objectivity of these comments, it is difficult to judge, since I've also encountered ELA teachers who gave stinging criticisms and are opposed to the CCSS. But if changes are made to the K–12 curriculum in any subject, there is going to be one of three possibilities. Changes can add value, they can be benign, or they can be destructive. Mathematics is a subject of logical connections, and the sequences of concepts taught in a particular area must have a heuristic purpose and should never be arbitrarily tampered with in the name of ideas such as providing "stands across content areas."

The NCTM has appropriately given some credit to CCSS for continuing an old practice where other content areas such as ELA and social studies assist with the essential vocabulary that is needed for comprehension in mathematics with the comment, "NCTM is encouraged by the standards' references to mathematical connections—both across content strands or categories and with contextual, real-world settings."[154]

But that credit came with a caveat. According to the NTCM:

*However, as with the mathematical practices, little explicit
attention is given to connections in the standards. Without
more focused attention on critical connections, such as
those between number or algebra and geometry, or among*

multiple representations of big mathematical ideas, the rich possibilities for mathematical connections in any taxonomy such as this one are likely to remain underdeveloped in assessments, instructional materials, and instruction. Likewise, because mathematics is more than applications and "real world" settings, the Common Core Standards should also encourage students and teachers to understand why they should be interested in or intrigued by the mathematical content itself.[155]

I've actually heard from one parent that her student's CCSS mathematics teacher gave her son's sixth-grade class an assignment to write an essay entitled, "My Favorite Number." When I requested more specifics, she sent me an e-mail containing the workbook page in figure 9.2.

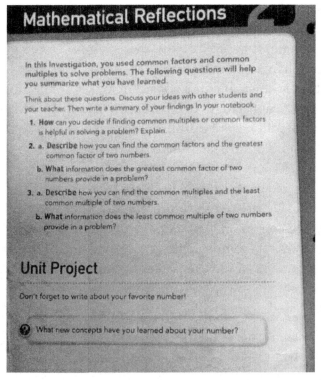

Figure 9.2

On reading this assignment, I couldn't help but think of physicist Richard Feynman, who won the Nobel Prize for his work in quantum electrodynamics. How would he as a student respond to this assignment? Here is Feynman in his own words:

> *I was terrible in English. I couldn't stand the subject. It seemed to me ridiculous to worry about whether you spelled something wrong or not, because English spelling is just a human convention — it has nothing to do with anything real, anything from nature. Any word can be spelled just as well a different way.*"[156]

My immediate reaction was this assignment could not have been written by a mathematics teacher. It occurred to me that such an assignment was too general for a mathematics class and was a waste of time for both mathematics teachers and for the students. It would most likely frustrate the middle- and lower-performing students.

If I wanted to infuse writing skills involving mathematics, depending on grade level and context, I would have given a subject-specific assignment such as:

1. Find the least common multiple (LCM) of 6 and 8. Give an explanation of each step.

Or, again depending on grade level, I might have offered one such as:

2. Find the greatest common factor (GCF) of 18 and 24. Give an explanation of each step.

Some students with Richard Feynman's ability would get the answer in their minds immediately and would be ready for the next question, dreading having to explain the process in written sentences. As a mathematics teacher, I see a value in developing verbal skills through proper use of grammar and syntax, but I would give more credit to the process of finding the LCM or the GCF than to the written explanations. I would not want to frustrate students as gifted as a Richard Feynman by having them waste time writing about their favorite number.

Perhaps the most damning of the NCTM's comments on the CCSS is about the kind of naiveté on one hand and arrogance on the other, on the part of the CCSS writing team, displayed in its insistence on "learning progressions." It is in this aspect that parents and teachers seem to have most frustrations. This is what the NCTM said on that matter: "Several learning progressions are overambitious and push the bounds of what is known from research, and others are superficial or underdeveloped."[157]

In mathematics, whether in arithmetic, algebra, geometry, trigonometry, or any area of the subject, it is essential that there is a seamless transition from one concept to the next. This is what makes mathematics enjoyable. On the other hand, a single conceptual misstep can cause permanent discouragement and frustration for the best of students, and can create deadly learning misconceptions for the middle- and lower-performing students.

One of the most disconcerting obstacles for students learning in any discipline is to learn an algorithm or a practical method of procedure, and then be required to unlearn that same algorithm later. The NCTM elaborated on this aspect of the CCSS learning progressions:

> We cannot send a message to teachers, parents, and students that an efficient algorithm that is already well understood and mastered by a child must be unlearned in a favor of a single mathematical algorithm chosen by this writing team. Of concern is that the current statement invites assessment of a student's ability to use the exact steps in an algorithm that someone else had in mind—not an ability to execute the required computation.[158]

The writing team leader Jason Zimba must take responsibility for this anomaly. It feeds into a flawed pedagogical practice, where we have a few incompetent teachers insisting that students must do a problem the teachers' way. An effective pedagogical approach must take into account the various learning styles of the students in a class. The ultimate goal of mathematics is problem solving. One step of George Polya's four-step process for problem solving is as follows:

"Devise a Plan: There are many ways to attack a problem and decide what plan is appropriate for the particular problem you are solving."[159] Among the planning strategies Polya suggested are:

Make a table or chart
Draw a sketch
Use inductive reasoning
Guess and check
Trial and error
Work backward
Look for a pattern
Write an equation and solve it.[160]

These are strategies students should be encouraged to employ, depending on the problem and learning style. Polya's approach is effective because it involves choices for the students to plan the solution for a particular problem. A teacher's insistence on a single approach to problem solving dictated by the curriculum stifles imagination, limits flexibility, and most deadly of all alienates students whose learning styles are not in synchrony with the dictates of the particular method insisted on by the teacher. In practice, a problem may require using more than one of Polya's strategies. The "look for a pattern" strategy, for example, is one I've stressed throughout this letter. It was pattern observation and other strategies that enabled mathematician Alan Turing to crack the Enigma Code, which was pivotal to the Allied victory over the Germans in World War II.[161] But it would be ridiculous to restrict all students to using only pattern observation in mathematics problems.

In chapter 6, I pointed out that one of the most effective attributes of the metric system is that has a base ten or decimalized structure, a quality that contributes to its ease of use. Here is what the NCTM had to say about this aspect of the CCSS:

In the early childhood grades, there are two places where student understanding is likely to be sacrificed in a rush for rote responses that would lose the intended building blocks of understanding. In the Kindergarten base-ten numeration section, an expectation of full understanding that "10 is both a unit of 10 and 10 ones" or that the 8 in 89 represents 8 tens will be premature for many children. While students can learn to provide cued responses, these are often not based on the understanding currently described in the Kindergarten narrative.[162]

In this regard, the CCSS would have had some advantage if we lived in a metric system environment. In the current USCS environment, the CCSS is obviously doing more harm than good. Without the cultural and cognitive underpinnings of the base ten structured metric system, we can only imagine the frustrations experienced by the middle- and lower-performing students, as well as by parents who encounter these frustrations first hand.

In yet another area where the CCSS could have some success in a metric culture, the learning progression for decimals, the NCTM made the following uncomplimentary statement:

Another example is that the learning progression for decimal concepts and computation is ill conceived. The decimal concepts presented in grade 4 are insufficient to prepare students to perform all four operations with decimals as expected in grade 5. More attention to decimal concepts and computation is needed throughout grades 4–7.[163]

Since the CCSS was "not yet finished," when it was accepted as the new standard at federal level, it is obvious that there was little or no collaboration with the NTCM before the actual rollout. Teachers and students encountered many errors in CCSS tests; homework problems that frustrated both students and parents must be attributed to the hurried nature of the rollout, with little or no time for meticulous editing and curriculum analysis. Such errors are part of what led to the NCTM's reflective skepticism.

9.3 Common Core and Precollege Preparation in Mathematics

I have argued that if we had the metric system in this country, the utilization of the Celsius scale would provide students with early familiarity with negative numbers and the key to beginning algebra before kindergarten. I tried to make the case that Russian children's experience of negative numbers in the winter months each year is the reason why Russians students can start algebra as early as the first grade. I have also pointed out that the CCSS introduces negative numbers for the first time in grade 6. After this introduction, negative numbers remain classroom abstractions because there is no environmental or real-life reinforcement for cognitive retention. It was shown that the Canadian mathematics curriculum utilizes the negative-number environment in that country to introduce algebraic concepts very early in their K–12 curriculum. That utilization accomplishes two things. First, Canada has always scored in the top ten on the PISA test. Second, Canadian students have the opportunity to complete calculus as part of their precollege preparation in high schools. Canada is a British Commonwealth country and, like Great Britain and other Commonwealth countries such as Australia, New Zealand, and Jamaica, students complete calculus in high school.

The lead writer for Common Core mathematics, Jason Zimba, has acknowledged that Common Core mathematics does not prepare students to reach calculus in the American high school. In fact, regarding a full course in algebra, Zimba said that will not happen until high school. According Sarah Carr's "Hechinger Report" in *The Advocate*:

> *Jason Zimba, a professor of physics and math at Bennington College in Vermont and lead writer of the math standards, says they include "an awful lot of algebra before eighth grade," even though the first full course doesn't come until high school.*[164]

Before the launch of the CCSS, many public schools in New York City had selected students completing a full algebra I course in the eighth grade. Such students were able to take advanced placement calculus in high school, giving them a solid head start for college mathematics. In this regard, the CCSS is specifically disruptive and regressive. But what I found most startling, if not shocking, is that the CCSS mathematics does nothing to prepare students to take calculus at the high school level. Sarah Carr went on to state that:

> *[Jason] Zimba also acknowledges that ending with the*
> *Common Core in high school could preclude students from*
> *attending elite colleges. In many cases, the Core is not*
> *aligned with the expectations at the collegiate level. "If you*
> *want to take calculus your freshman year in college, you*
> *will need to take more mathematics than is in the Common*
> *Core," Zimba said.*[165]

In other words, CCSS does nothing to lower calculus from university level into the American high school curriculum, thus falling far short of our Canadian counterparts. Even more startling is the fact that in a question-and-answer exchange with Dr. Sandra Stotsky in a meeting at the Massachusetts Board of Elementary and Secondary Education on March 23, 2010, Jason Zimba stated explicitly that Common Core mathematics is not sufficient to prepare students for the STEM program, and certainly is not designed to get students into selective colleges.[166]

Had I been at that meeting, I would have asked Dr. Zimba three questions: First, what is the real purpose of the CCSS mathematics beyond evaluating teachers and schools on the basis of test scores? Second, why should the CCSS not be seen as "failure by design" scheme, as suggested by Diane Ravitch, to create more privately managed charter schools? Third, why is the CCSS mathematics curriculum a better alternative than the NCTM process standards?

The mathematics lead writer implicitly suggests that CCSS mathematics is a truncation of the NTCM standards. In practice, it is killing the joy and excitement that is the motivational vehicle for children to embrace mathematics with enthusiasm, satisfaction, pleasure, and passion, accompanied by a zest to learn more.

It is a recorded fact that Finland is one of the countries that is consistently in the top ten on the PISA tests. "Satisfaction and pleasure" are words included in one of Finland's objectives for grades 1–2 mathematics: "Pupils will learn to concentrate, listen, communicate, and develop their thinking: they will derive satisfaction and pleasure from understanding and solving problems."[167]

Compare this aspect of Finland's model with American students' and parents' horrifying experiences with CCSS mathematics. The complaint that very capable students are in tears with their CCSS mathematics homework assignments is anathema to how mathematics should be taught. With the CCSS, students encounter math problems from textbooks and testing companies that even teachers don't understand. It has created a number of horror stories of children being frustrated and discouraged and teachers being aggravated because their job performances are being measured by weird anomalies that can only lead to negative evaluations.

9.4 The Common Core Standard from School and Community Perspectives

When New York Commissioner of Education John B. King Jr. resigned and was immediately employed as a senior advisor to DE Secretary Arne Duncan, the CCSS was left in place as the operative curriculum in New York State, as well as in forty-five other states and the District of Columbia. We have read the critique of the CCSS curriculum by the NCTM. We have heard from the lead writer of the CCSS mathematics, Dr. Jason Zimba, about lowered expectations for Common Core mathematics, but how have school district administrators reacted to the CCSS?

In an article appearing in *Newsday*, it was reported that over 500 principals across New York State have joined the movement against the newly imposed testing under the CCSS. These seasoned educators, in an open letter written to the parents across New York State, opposed the tests on the basis that they amounted to "no clear benefit to the students."[168]

In chapter 8, we mentioned that the CCSS was neither field-tested nor piloted before being implemented. Here is part of the letter as reported by the *Newsday* article:

> *"Under current conditions, we fear that the hasty implementation of unpiloted assessments will continue to cause more harm than good," read the letter drafted last month. It has 3,160 signatures, including 248 principals from Long Island.*[169]

Let us now learn about the frustrating experiences of award-winning high school principal Carol Burris, who participated in writing the open letter mentioned above. We met her before in chapter 8.

An article in the *Washington Post* entitled "A Ridiculous Common Core Test for First Graders," asked the question, "Why are some kids crying when they do homework these days?" This question about homework takes us to the heart of the problem with the CCSS. One can only imagine the frustration of parents who are supervising their children's homework. But other than homework, what is really going on in the mathematics classroom? Horror stories of frustrations abound, and for this we turn to Principal Carol Burris of South Side High School in New York. But first let's peruse a part of her curriculum vitae to authenticate why she deserves to be heard:

> *She [Carol Burris] was named New York's 2013 High School Principal of the Year by the School Administrators Association of New York and the National Association of Secondary School Principals, and in 2010, tapped as the 2010 New York State Outstanding Educator by the School Administrators Association of New York State.*[170]

Here is Principal Burris's description of an incident that occurred in her school:

> *My speech teacher came to see me. She was both angry and distraught. In her hand was her six-year-old's math test. On the top of it was written, "Topic 2, 45%." On the bottom*

*were the words, "Copyright @ Pearson Education." After I
got over my horror that a first-grader would take a multiple-
choice test with a percent-based grade, I started to look at the
questions.*[171]

After describing the anomalies in the first test question, she made
the astonishing statement: "My assistant principal for mathematics
was not sure what the question was asking. How could pennies be a
part of a cup?"[172]

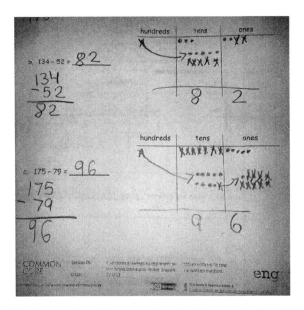

Figure 9.3: *Source: http://www.nationalreview.com/article/373840/
ten-dumbest-common-core-problems-alec-torres*

But there is more. Here is Burris's description of another question
on the test that was so complex that even a calculus teacher had
difficulty finding the answer:

*Then there is Question No. 12. Would (or should) a 6 year
old understand the question, "Which is a related subtraction
sentence?" My nephew's wife, who teaches Calculus,*

was stumped by that one. Finally, think about the level
of sophistication required to answer the multiple-choice
question in No. 8, which asks students to "Circle the number
sentence that is true" from a list of four.[173]

In an article entitled "The Ten Dumbest Common Core Questions," by Alec Torres in the National Review, two of the questions intended for third grade, as shown in figures 9.3 and 9.4, were listed with comments. In the first problem the students are assigned a regular subtraction problem. "Not willing to ruin addition alone, educators take aim at subtraction as well, forcing students to make visual representations of numbers in columns."[174]

Can you imagine the likes of gifted students such as Nobel Prize for physics winner Richard Feynman in this class?

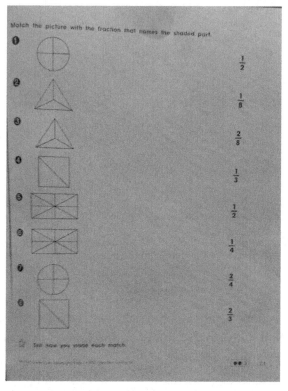

Figure 9.4: *Source: http://www.nationalreview.com/article/373840/*
ten-dumbest-common-core-problems-alec-torres

Here is the other problem (figure 9.4) with accompanying comments. This error is reflective of the effects of the hurried nature of the rollout of the CCSS. Not only was it neither field-tested nor piloted, but it was neither properly edited nor proofread.

This third-grade Common Core–compliant question asks students to match the shaded geometrical figures with their corresponding fractions. "Problem is, the figures aren't shaded."[175]

Math questions such as these were constructed by a publishing company. One cannot help but ask the question: who were the mathematics education professionals hired as test creators and editors to the publishers? How were they recruited? And why should a publishing company, rather than a consortium of mathematics teachers, be given authority to construct test questions or contents for over forty-five states? With a carefully selected group of mathematics teachers, errors like the one in the second problem above would have been discovered in the proofreading process. These hastily composed tests are causing havoc in schools, and yet the publishing company has made its profits.

If schools across the country are dealing with the same kinds of test and curricular shortcomings as the ones mentioned by writer Alex Torres and principal Carol Burris, this has to be bad news for the future of the CCSS. In expressing concerns for the students, for the teachers, and for the parents involved, Burris was as emphatic as she was specific. Here is her perspective as a professional educator:

> When one actually examines the standards and the tests like the sample I provided, it quickly becomes apparent why young students are crying when they do their homework and telling their parents they do not want to go to school. Many New York children are simply not developmentally ready to do the work. Much of the work is confusing. When you add the pressure under which teachers find themselves to quickly implement the standards and prepare students for standardized testing, it becomes clear why New York parents are expressing outrage at forums across the state.[176]

On the matter of losing a whole generation of students, a concern I have previously mentioned, principal Burris said the following:

> *It is time for New York State to heed, at the very least,*
> *the New York State United Teachers' call for a three-year*
> *moratorium on high-stakes testing, thus providing time*
> *for New York to reexamine its reforms, and change course.*
> *New York, sadly, has been a canary in the Common Core*
> *coal mine, and if we do not heed the danger a generation of*
> *students will be lost.*[177]

That last sentence in the statement succinctly sums up the most ominous aspects of the CCSS. Rather than ensuring that educational policies are structured to motivate and educate students through satisfaction and pleasure in their schoolwork, we are allowing educational novices to make policies that simultaneously evaluate teachers while intimidating students, destroying public school education, and the most ominous of all, destroying the future of a whole generation of students, in favor of promoting the construction of privately managed charter schools. If we fail to let professional educators do what they are trained to do, rather than being dictated to by publishing companies incentivized by profits, we will be complicit in allowing the invidious corruption of our education system. The suspicion that the construction of the CCSS was guided by a "Failure by Design" conspiratorial paradigm is clearly justified.

We have previously mentioned some state governors' negative reaction to the CCSS. But what were the views of New York Governor Andrew Cuomo? It was on his watch that Common Core was implemented in New York State. He was aware of his state's education commissioner's advocacy. All indications are that he was originally in full support of the CCSS. But in a pre-election statement, he seemed to have had second thoughts. According to the *Washington Post*, here is one of Governor Cuomo's ex post facto statements:

> *The way Common Core has been managed by the Board of*
> *Regents is flawed. There is too much uncertainty, confusion*
> *and anxiety. Parents, students, and teachers need the best*

> *education reforms — which include Common Core and*
> *teacher evaluations — but they also need a rational system*
> *that is well administered. We will assemble a panel that*
> *includes education experts and Members of the Legislature*
> *to make recommendations for corrective action by the end of*
> *this session on how Common Core should be implemented.*[178]

As can be observed, he is sticking to his approval of "Common Core Teacher Evaluations." That is the nature of politics. This statement was made while running for a second term for governor of New York. Here, he wants to "assemble a panel that includes education experts," and "members of the legislator to make recommendations for corrective action." Will Governor Andrew Cuomo revolutionize mathematics and science education in New York State?

9.5 *Where Do We Go from Here?*

Initiatives previous to the CCSS, such as "No Child Left Behind" and NMAP, were well intended and may even have succeeded in some instances. "Race to the Top" seems to be a mixed bag. On the one hand there are the positive aspects of the limited STEM program, but on the other, the nationwide CCSS amounts to a conspiratorial squandering of federal funds. Reports from the field indicate that the CCSS is an unmitigated disaster that could have serious downside effects on K–12 mathematics for years to come. In this respect, I believe that Secretary of Education Arne Duncan's support and promotion of the CCSS was a specific disservice to the future of mathematics and science education in the United States, to the country, and to the president whom he advises. The squandering of billions of dollars in federal funds to states that implemented the CCSS at a time when it was not yet finished did more to enrich publishers and software companies than to improve mathematics and science education in our country. It most certainly will provide a charter school bonanza for profit-seeking entrepreneurs. In this regard, as indicated before, no one has made the case for abolishing the Department of Education more vividly than Secretary

Duncan. Unfortunately, when the final evaluation is made about the CCSS, Secretary Duncan will be long gone from office.

In the wake of Arne Duncan's legacy, this country will need a mathematics education visionary who will put the United States on a path to excellence second to none in the world. Because of the foundational of nature of mathematics, all the sciences depend on and need this unique subject. Mathematics is a reservoir of knowledge that constitutes the purest form of truth. Here is an apt description of the subject from one the greatest mathematicians of the twentieth century, Bertrand Russell:

> Mathematics, rightly viewed, possesses not only truth, but supreme beauty—a beauty cold and austere, like that of sculpture, without appeal to any part of our weaker nature, without the gorgeous trappings of painting or music, yet sublimely pure, and capable of a stern perfection such as only the greatest art can show."[179]

The learning process of mathematics is dependent on learning styles. Learning the Common Core way is disastrous precisely because it ignores students' learning styles. Effective learning is best when the delivery of instruction is constructed on heuristic building blocks and logical sequencing of concepts in a succession of seamlessly connected steps. Nobel laureate Richard Feynman could survive American education because he taught himself high school mathematics, and then some. But the Feynmans of the world are very different from the average student, and they are certainly different from those who are middle and lower performers. It takes meticulous curriculum construction and creative pedagogy by experienced professional educators to impart to young children the joy, appreciation, and pleasure inherent in the grasping of mathematical concepts.

For those of us who have a professional and esthetic appreciation of mathematics from a content and pedagogical perspective, the idea that children should be in tears over homework exercises and test questions, that teachers should be distressed by questions formulated by a book company, that teacher evaluations should be based on the passing results of standards-based tests filled with anomalies is as disheartening as it is disturbing. "Failure by design" must be stopped in its tracks. If something is not promptly done to remove the horrible educational cancer that is the CCSS, it will continue to metastasize and jeopardize the future of our country. Teachers, students, and parents are becoming victims of the government we elect. As Diane Ravitch puts it, "for the past dozen years, ill-advised federal and state policies have rained down on students, teachers, principals, and schools."[180]

In the interest of achieving value-added mathematics education reform in this country, and to avoid further loss of a whole generation of American mathematics students, three suggestions seem prudent. First, the American people should be resolute in the demand to stop the Common Core State Standards now, and to temporarily return to the most recently updated NTCM standards. Second, we should appoint a mathematics education visionary, and begin to dismantle the United States Department of Education and merge it with the Department of Commerce. This would save billions of dollars for taxpayers while getting substantive education reform products from a department that has a history of promoting specific improvements to the education of America's children. Third, with the amalgamation of both departments, the mathematics education visionary should revisit Secretary of Commerce Maurice Stans's letter to the Congress in 1968, which accompanied the report "A Metric America: A Decision Whose Time Has Come," with a resolve to implement his recommendation, "That early priority be given to educate every American schoolchild and the public at large to think in metric terms."

Temporary return to the NTCM standards should be immediately accompanied by putting together a consortium of mathematics teaching professionals from the membership of the NTCM. Armed with content knowledge and specializations in curriculum design and pedagogy, they can set to work collaboratively to reconstruct a new set of standards consistent with a metric system environment. They should be given broad latitudinal support to study the curricula of the countries belonging to the Organization for Economic Co-operation and Development (OECD) that are in the top ten on the PISA test. As was done in the Sputnik era, when college-level mathematics concepts were introduced at the high school level, steps should be taken to revolutionize elementary school mathematics by infusing algebra into that curriculum. With a five-billion-dollar budget and a ten-year phasing-in of the metric system, America would be on its way to unchallenged supremacy in mathematics, science, and engineering.

One way of rescuing the current generation of students from the ravages of the CCSS is to structure the mathematics curriculum so that current students transitioning to American high schools who show extraordinary aptitude in mathematics can take and complete both algebra and geometry by the end of the ninth grade. The rationale for this is that except for knowing how to solve simple equations and understanding ratio and proportion, algebra is not a prerequisite for geometry. As a student in Jamaica, I studied algebra and geometry simultaneously and easily passed the University of London General Certificate of Education (GCE) Ordinary Level Exam. When I was a mathematics teacher at Evander Childs High School, Bronx, New York, I recommended that several students take both algebra and geometry in one year in grade 9, and they passed the New York State Regents Exams in both subjects with scores in the top 90s. This initiative gave these students one full year of acceleration in high school mathematics. After taking intermediate algebra and trigonometry in the tenth grade, they went on to pre-calculus in the eleventh grade, and were able to complete calculus in the twelfth grade. If you'll permit me to brag a little, I still have in my possession a letter of commendation from the NAACP, received at Evander Childs High School, when my eleventh-grade mathematics class of twenty-seven students all passed the New York State Regents Examination. This outcome was considered extraordinary because at the time Evander was considered an inner-city school. The award letter specified that my accomplishment was the first in eighteen years at this high school. I wouldn't pretend to be as good as Jaime Escalante, (about whom more will be said in chapter11) of the movie *Stand and Deliver*, but this was one of the highlights of my teaching career.

In the next chapter, we'll discuss the role of parents, as homeschoolers, in the education of their children. As enhancements to the regular mathematics curriculum, a number of value-added enrichment activities in mathematics education will be offered. From experience, I can attest that these activities and undertakings have proven to bring enrichment, encouragement, excitement, and pleasure to motivate young children to experience the world of discrete and continuous mathematics.

PART III

THE ROLE OF PARENTS IN MATHEMATICS AND SCIENCE EDUCATION

CHAPTER 10:

The Importance of Parental Involvement in K–12 Education

In a Time magazine article entitled "Why Parenting Is More Important than Schools,"[181] Annie Murphy Paul reported on a new study showing that "Parental involvement matters more for performance than schools." She pointed out that this doesn't necessarily mean going to Parent Teacher Association (PTA) meetings but made the important point that "students spend less than 15 percent of the calendar year in school."[182] The chart in figure 10.1 gives us a close approximation of the distribution of the calendar year in school time, sleep time, and parent-community time.

Since this distribution obviously occurs after the child begins school, if we extrapolate to prekindergarten time distribution, then the time the student spends with parents outside of sleep time is 67 percent of the calendar year. Part of the reason I'm addressing this letter to parents is to invite a sharpened awareness of the vital role they can play in the education of American children. Figure 10.1 tells us that beginning with kindergarten, schools are responsible for the formal, structural, and organized education of children for only 14 percent of the calendar year. The quality of how 53 percent home and community times is spent can have a profound influence on the educational outcomes for the children. Constructive utilization of this time can be a powerful and productive supplement to school time. Recreation time can add value to education by engaging youngsters in activities that they can enjoy while enriching their minds. But after you've done your part, it is reasonable to expect that the institutions responsible for the formal education of your children will reciprocate by engaging real professionals to carry out the task and by justifying prudent allocation of taxpayers' money. Let us dispense with the notion that K–12 education is free. It takes a lot of taxpayers to pay for the multibillions in dollars that are expended on education each year in our country.

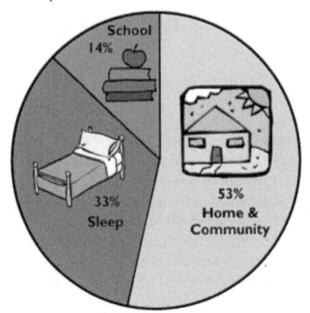

Figure 10.1: *Source: http://www.nap.edu/openbook.php?record_id=9853&page=26*

This leads again into what I've said before, that it is not unreasonable to expect that if the United States continues to lead the world in money spent per student on education, then we should demand nothing less than that our country lead the world in mathematics and science education. But what if our government does nothing that is effective? What if the lobbyists and exploitative educational pretenders continue to prevail? Then parental power needs to assert itself. There are several productive steps that parents can take to improve the education of our children in mathematics and science. You will need to be activists on the one hand, and on the other to engage your youngsters in productive activities during the time spent with parents and community. The following is a list of suggestions.

10.1. Community Organizing with Other Parents

Organize community groups or coalitions like the kind we have seen in the State of New York, which demanded and got the resignation of the education commissioner who was a Common Core advocate. Be relentless in contacting or writing letters to your congressmen and congresswomen as well as state representatives to urge them to abandon the CCSS through legislation. Persistence can be enormously effective. In chapter 9, I pointed out that Governor Andrew Cuomo was forced to react to parental pressure by reversing himself from outright support of the CCSS to saying that it is a flawed reform product.

We read the call for a moratorium on the CCSS from the likes of high school principal Carol Burris and we can only hope her call is heeded. But if we get such a moratorium, then what? Obviously, the schools and states involved must default to the pre-CCSS curriculum. As we have meticulously explored in this letter, this will not fix the problems we are experiencing in mathematics and science education. There is a void in the old curriculum caused by the US Customary System (USCS). As we have argued, this void can be filled only by phasing out the USCS while phasing in the metric system.

Your congressional and state representatives should be made aware or be reminded of the pitfalls accompanying past attempts to change our measurement system. For example, when the liter suddenly appeared at the gas pump, Americans rightly objected to the new and unknown measure, because unscrupulous gas station owners use the sudden change from gallons to liter to jack up prices, making gasoline more expensive in liters than it would have been in gallons. The simple remedy for this is to have each gas station post the equivalent price per gallon as a deterrent to price gouging.

10.2 Getting the Metric System in School Districts across the Country

Get involved with the activities of the local school board. Attend meetings, and insist that school districts should work with book publishing companies to cease using USCS units in mathematics textbooks. Insist that each classroom have at least one Celsius thermometer as well as metric system tables on each classroom wall. Each classroom should have at least one meter stick, access to a metric trundle wheel (see figure 10.2), a scale for weight in grams, a micrometer, and measuring jars calibrated in liters. A meter stick, which is approximately 39 inches in length, is calibrated in centimeters (100 cm) and millimeters (1000 mm), and can be used to engage in various kinds of measurements of length, and to calculate area and volume in metric units. A micrometer, an instrument calibrated to measure small lengths to an accuracy of one-millionth of a meter, is more suited for science and can be uses to measure small lengths such as the diameter of a strand of hair or the thickness of a sheet of paper.

A scale calibrated in grams along with several weights representing multiples or submultiples of the gram can do more than weighing things. A scale is a great manipulative for teaching children about equations. As a mathematics teacher, I have introduced simple equations by bringing a scale to class to demonstrate to my students that "an equation is like a balance." If we add a metric weight to one side of the scale, we must add an equal metric weight to the other side to maintain the balance. The same goes for subtraction. If we take a metric weight from one side, we must take an equal metric weight from the other side to keep the balance. Keeping that balance, by adding, subtracting, multiplying, or dividing both sides of the equation by the same number, except zero, is the key to solution of simple algebraic equations. This would be a great way to encouraging thinking in metric to reinforce the four basic operations in elementary schools while getting acquainted with the method of solving simple equations.

Teachers are trained to be resourceful, and so they can create several activities to integrate these new classroom acquisitions into the curriculum. When you visit your school or attend parent-teacher conferences, be sure to ask about the availability of the metric manipulatives I've suggested. Effective schools and good teachers welcome constructive suggestions, particularly from informed parents.

Figure 10.2: *A meter trundle wheel.*
*Source: http://www.eaieducation.com/Product/533057/Trundle_Wheel_-_Metric.aspx?utm_*

10.3 Homeschooling with the Metric System

Whether or not you are homeschooling your children full time, get your child a meter stick, Celsius thermometer, metric weights, and a balance. You will note, as indicated before, that the meter stick is divided into 100 centimeters and 1000 millimeters. Get acquainted with the contents of your children's textbooks. Have them measure things around the house in metric, to get what I would call "metric sense." Have them observe that the centimeter is about the cross-section width (the diameter) of the average finger. Familiarity with liters and grams will have a cumulative cognitive effect. If your child's homework or textbook exercises are in USCS, have your child do at least some of the exercises a second time in metric, by using conversion tables such as in figure 6.12. Almost all the packages, boxes, and cans bought at grocery stores in the US have metric measures in grams or liters. As an option, you may also want to get, or share with a homeschooling parent group, a meter trundle wheel. This is a great instrument for measuring distances around the yard, in the park or playground, or on a hike or walk. You will have the ability to measure the distance in meters very easily, by rolling the trundle wheel where each revolution is one meter. For those of you who still think in miles, remember that 1000 meters is a kilometer, a kilometer is approximately 0.6 of a mile. With a trundle wheel, you can consult the Internet for instruction on how to use proportionality to find the height of a flagpole or a building by merely measuring the shadow of the flagpole or building, the shadow of a measurable rod, and the measure of the rod itself.

Gaining acquaintance with the Celsius scale is very easy with today's media capabilities. Since your television or radio station will give the temperature in Fahrenheit, have your children do a conversion to Celsius. My iPhone has a weather app that gives the temperature in both Fahrenheit (F) and Celsius (C). In the US, it defaults to the Fahrenheit scale, but with a touch of your finger, you can read the equivalent temperature in Celsius. Watch the weather reports on cable TV station *BBC World News*, where temperatures around the world and the US are given in Celsius. Organize a letter-writing campaign to all local television and radio stations to request that they give temperatures in both scales. I've observed that weather broadcasters, who are versed in the sciences, appreciate invitations to schools to be involved with science projects. Ask your school to invite the local TV weatherperson or the local TV or radio meteorologist to your school, and state the case why Celsius temperatures should be included in broadcasts.

By the way, if you and your family travel to Canada or any country where the temperatures are given in Celsius, and you don't have a cell phone or tablet, you may want to have an idea of how to quickly convert to the familiar Fahrenheit scale. To get a rough approximation, double the Celsius temperature and then add 32. For example, if the Celsius temperature is 20 degrees, the approximate Fahrenheit reading is $2 \times 20 + 32$, or 72 degrees. This comes from the scientific formula for conversion from Celsius to Fahrenheit. The formula is $F = \frac{9}{5}C + 32$, where F is for Fahrenheit and C is for Celsius. Note that the fraction $\frac{9}{5}$ is approximately equal to 2. Hence we can replace $\frac{9}{5}$ in the formula with 2, to get the approximation formula, $F \approx 2C + 32$. (The symbol for approximation is "$\approx$".)

The formula to convert from Fahrenheit to Celsius is $C = \frac{5}{9}(F - 32)$. To follow the order of operations, we must first do the calculation inside the parentheses. Therefore, a good approximation method of converting to Celsius from a Fahrenheit temperature is to first subtract 32 from the given Fahrenheit temperature, then take half of the answer, to get an approximation in Celsius. For example if we have a temperature of 68°F, the approximate Celsius temperature is $\frac{1}{2}(68 - 32)$, or $\frac{1}{2}$ of $36 \approx 18°C$. We take one-half, because the fraction $\frac{5}{9}$ is approximately ($\approx$) equal to $\frac{1}{2}$. In this case, the approximation formula is $C \approx \frac{1}{2}(F - 32)$. If the exact Celsius temperature were calculated we would get $C = \frac{5}{9}(F - 32)$ or 20°C. The difference is not significant for daily utilitarian purposes.

For the home-school parents, we will proceed to the next section, to explore a set of practical exercises in beginning algebra for first-, second-, and third-grade students.

10.4 Simple Algebra Concepts for First, Second and Third Graders.

The purpose of this section is to provide home-school parents with some convenient and available tools to help their youngsters not only to get acquainted with negative integers but to offer a constructive beginning to the four basic operations on these numbers through intuition. To accommodate different learning styles, other approaches will be provided in the postscripts of this letter. Since addition is the key operation for understanding multiplication, subtraction, and division, the focus in this section will be on addition of integers.

Before getting to the addition exercises, it is prudent to state that subtraction is defined in terms of addition. A formal definition of subtraction and how to subtraction one number from another will be given later in postscript P.S. 4.

We will now explore addition of integers, using the number line.

You will recall figure 3.1 below, from chapter 3, which you were asked to keep in mind.

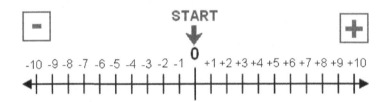

Figure 3.1 (Taken from chapter 3): *Source: http://www.green-planet-solar-energy.com/support-files/number-line*

In the number line below, figure 10.3, you'll note that only the negative numbers have signs. When a non-zero number has no sign, it is understood to be a positive number. This is because in the daily use of numbers we only use signs when a number is negative. As such, it is acceptable to use a number line where only the negative numbers have signs. Also it is useful to observe that we count to the left as we get progressively negative, and we count to the right as we get progressively positive.

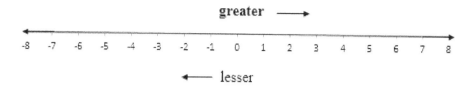

greater ⟶

-8 -7 -6 -5 -4 -3 -2 -1 0 1 2 3 4 5 6 7 8

⟵ lesser

Figure 10.3: *Number lines, similar to figure 10.3, are available on the Internet at the website: http://themathworksheetsite.com/numline.html.*

Let us now use the number line for the operation of addition with the following four pairs of numbers. Using lower single-digit numbers rather than higher single-digit or double-digit numbers will make it easy for elementary school children.

1. $(+3) + (+4)$

2. $(-3) + (-4)$

3. $(+6) + (-2)$

4. $(-6) + (+2)$

Since addition is commutative, to get the answer or the sum in each problem, we can start each problem by counting from zero with either of the numbers in the pair. If a number is positive, we count to the right, and if it is negative, we count to the left. After the second number is counted, the arrowhead should point to the answer. To give emphasis to the **commutative property of addition**, where order is not important, there will be two graphics for each problem, showing that we can start the addition process with either of the two numbers.

1. **Add $(+3) + (+4)$**

   In figure 10.4a, we start from 0 and count 3 spaces going right, then from this point, count 4 spaces going right, to arrive at the answer, which is 7 or +7. In figure 10.4b, start from 0 and count 4 spaces to the right, then from this point, count 3 more spaces to the right to arrive at the answer, which is 7 or +7. Thus $(+3) + (+4) = +7$ or 7.

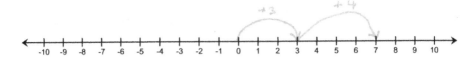

Figure 10.4a

Figure 10.4b

2. **Add (-3) + (-4)**
   In figure 10.4c, start at 0 and count 3 spaces to the left, continue counting 4 more paces to the left, to arrive at the answer, which is −7. In figure 10.4d, start at 0 and count 4 spaces to the left, then continue counting 3 spaces to the left, to arrive at the answer, which is −7. Thus (−3) + (−4) = −7.

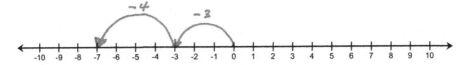

Figure 10.4c

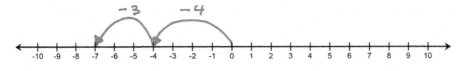

Figure 10.4d

3. **Add (-6) + (+2)**
   In figure 10.4e, start at 0 and count 6 spaces going left, then count 2 spaces going right, to arrive at the answer, which is −4. In figure 10.4f, start at 0 and count 2 spaces going right, then count 6 spaces going left, to arrive at the answer, which is −4. Thus (−6) + (+2) = −4

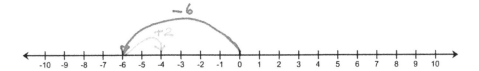

Figure 10.4e

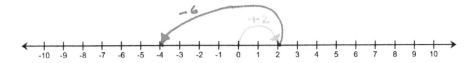

Figure 10.4f

4. **Add (+6) + (-2)**

    In figure 10.4g, start at 0 and count 2 spaces going left, then count 6 spaces going right, to arrive at the answer, which is 4 or +4. In figure 10.4h, start at 0 and count 6 spaces going right, then count 2 spaces going left, to arrive at the answer, which is 4 or +4. Thus (+6) + (−2) = +4.

Figure 10.4g

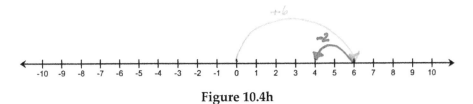

Figure 10.4h

Two patterns will emerge from these graphical solutions. One is concerned with addition of two numbers with the same sign, and the other with adding two numbers with opposite signs. These patterns are as follows:

1. When adding two numbers from one side of the number line, the answer is on that same side of the number line.
2. When adding two numbers from different sides of the number line, the answer is on the side containing the number that is farthest from zero.

You can observe these two patterns as formalized algebraic propositions for addition of signed numbers in the postscripts of this letter i.e. P.S. 5.

In postscripts P.S. 4 and P.S. 5 we'll explore other approaches to the addition of signed numbers. This is prudent because it is axiomatic that no two students have exactly the same learning style. These different approaches are designed to accommodate learning style variations.

10.5 How to Help Your Child Get Excellent Grades

Getting excellent grades is perhaps the most effective motivating factor in the life of a student, with the dividend of forging mutual pride between parent and child.

You can give your child a great head start, in any subject, by asking your child's teacher for a copy of the course outline, at or before the start of the school year. Each year, an efficiently run school district will have plans in place for what is to be taught in all classes for the coming calendar year. This outline should contain the progressive sequence of concepts in a course of study for the term or semester. Armed with the course outline, you can keep your child ahead of the class through use of the Internet. If you know what concept your child will be taught the coming school day, then you and your child can have a preview on the Internet, thus giving the child a great head start. In fact you can utilize part of the weekend time to prepare for the coming week.

I cannot overstress the value of using the Internet for the teaching/learning process. Any topic or concept is available with multiple perspectives, particularly on YouTube (www.youtube.com.) Here you'll find lessons on all of the concepts mentioned in the course outline. By beginning the search with the words "How to"—as in, "How to use two-color counters to multiply integers"—the search engine's algorithms will locate various presentations. One word of caution: you'll see different people with different presentation methodologies for the same concept. You'll want to select those that have clarity. Clarity is the essential ingredient for heuristic building of mathematical knowledge. For those parents who may not have a computer at home, there is Internet access at most if not all public libraries.

Another useful website is the Kahn Academy at www. kahnacademy.org. At this website, you'll find lessons on all subjects. One word of caution with the Kahn Academy is that each lesson is given by one instructor and tends to cater to a singular learning style. Whether you use YouTube or the Kahn Academy, your child will benefit enormously by watching the lesson online at home before doing the same lesson at school. The child may not understand everything, but the preview will provide a powerful receptive foundation for grasping a concept before class. This is a sound strategy to strengthen understanding while maximizing the child's pride in mathematics by getting a high grade on the report card.

Being involved in your children's education will pay dividends not only for the child's future, but also for you as a parent, through your own reeducation. It is my hope that you too as a parent will discover or rediscover the joy of mathematics. You will be contributing to making our country a scientific juggernaut for centuries to come.

PART IV

WRAPPING IT ALL UP

CHAPTER 11:
Conclusion

In this letter to you, the parents of the United States, I have taken you through the serious, urgent, and persistent problem of underperformance in mathematics and science by American fifteen-year-old students on the PISA test series. I have also stated the serious ramifications for our country in terms of shortages of skilled American candidates to fill job vacancies in mathematics, science, and engineering technology. In addition, I've discussed the initiatives of the two most recent presidents of the US, who took steps intended to effectuate improvements. One focused on preparing students to take and to succeed in algebra, while the other focused on a broader theme to engender improvement in mathematics and science education. We also informed you that the first president of the United States, George Washington, and some of his successors had the tremendous foresight and were fervent proponents of total conversion to the metric system.

I also wrote about the spurious nature of the Common Core State Standards and the inherent issues with parents, teachers, principals, and students. I have suggested that as parents, you must voice your abhorrence that people who call themselves educators are exploiting the availability of federal funds for personal financial enhancements. Indeed, there are already parents, teachers, education professionals, and organizations of educational professionals that have been speaking out and protesting the Common Core State Standards. Governors who initially support CCSS are now having second thoughts, based on public negative reaction. We have seen a skilled lawyer who has specific interest in taxpayer-funded charter schools use his position as commissioner of education of New York State to aggressively defend the CCSS. He did this though there was a failure to follow standards of scientific exactitude and minimum protocols for new programs that needed to be met before implementation of a nationwide initiative.

I have tried to present my suggestion for improvement, with a rationale based on evidence, as to the root cause of why fifteen-year-old US students cannot compete with their international counterparts. I have demonstrated the symbiotic relationship between the metric system, which includes the Celsius scale, and mathematics education as well as science education.

I believe there is an urgency for a solution to the paradox in which we find ourselves, that the US spends more money per student than any other country in the world, and yet it lags far behind too many of its international counterparts in math and science education. If the problem is not solved this time, we will continue to be dependent on other countries for our best scientists, mathematicians, and engineers. As mentioned in the introduction, the likes of Bill Gates of the Microsoft Corporation have petitioned congress for immigration reform so that the United States can employ more highly skilled foreign-born workers. According to him, if more of such workers are not imported, "American companies simply will not have the talent they need to innovate and compete." He went on to say that "Our higher education system doesn't produce enough scientists and engineers to meet the needs of the economy."[183] Are we as Americans supposed to stand idly by while the means for improvement is within our grasp? There is an old saying attributed to English writer John Heywood that states that "There is no one so blind as he who refuses to see." The first president of our country foresaw the efficacy of the metric system and its essential necessity for commerce and education. The Congress of the United States had the solution within their grasp, if only they had heeded the advice of forward-looking Commerce Secretary Maurice Stans, who stated explicitly that American children needed to be educated in metric. They passed "The Metric Act of 1975," but lobbyists prevailed, and the highly recommended phasing-in component was deliberately left out.

When was the last time you elected a lobbyist to represent you? And yet, especially these days, there is hardly any congressional legislation that is not influenced by hard-driving lobbyists whose interests involve profit at the expense of the public good.

11.1 Flawed Perceptions about Teachers and Teacher Quality.

When the 2003 PISA results were published, showing that the United States had placed below twenty industrialized countries in mathematics, the then Deputy Secretary of Education Eugene Hickok stated, "We need to get young people interested in math and science at a younger age...We need more qualified math teachers."[184]

I couldn't agree more on the idea of getting young people interested in math and science at a younger age. On the issue of "more qualified math teachers," I would argue from experience that the teacher in any school system is as good as the environment from which the students originate. This means that teachers will do better with students who are prepared and have the necessary prerequisites before coming to school or before moving through the hierarchy or successions of classes.

After the 2006 PISA results, when the United States placed twenty-fifth in the world, the Exxon Corporation took up the cause under a caption entitled, "Lets Solve This." If you type the words "Exxon math science commercial" in the YouTube search engine, you'll find a number of presentations with voiceovers. In addition to the one discussed in the introduction, there is this one:

*When you take a closer look at the best schools in the
world, you'll see they all have something very interesting
in common. They have teachers with a deeper knowledge of
the subject. As a result, their students achieve at a higher
level.*[185]

I take some issue with this statement, suggesting that the
best schools have teachers who have "a deeper knowledge" of
mathematics. This cannot be a universal truth, since all teachers who
meet state qualification criteria are obligated to adhere to the elements
of the curriculum in a particular school. In the case of the CCSS, the
curriculum is an imposition that is restrictive in terms of what teachers
are required to teach.

As for the idea that depth of knowledge of the subject on the part
of teachers is a definitive determinant of school effectiveness, I disagree
vehemently. Two of the best high schools in the world are in the New
York City School System. They are the Bronx High School of Science,
from which the likes of astrophysicist Neil deGrasse Tyson graduated,
and Stuyvesant High School. These two schools have more graduates
who are Nobel laureates than most universities.[186] They are among "the
best schools in the world," not because of the teachers, but because the
students have been tested for the prerequisite knowledge before they can
be admitted. Passing an admission test is mandatory for admission. On
the other hand, all teachers in New York City have the same qualification
and certifications as those who teach at these two schools. Teachers are
not specially selected to these schools because they have a "deeper
knowledge of the subject" as the Exxon commercial would have you
believe. All certified New York City teachers must be able to teach at
these two schools. At least, that was the case beginning in the 1970s
when I obtained certification as a mathematics teacher in the New York
City school system. It continued to be the case beginning in the 1980s,
when I was subsequently certified as assistant principal—supervisor of
mathematics in that system. The fact is that most so called "best schools"
are more selective of the students they admit than the teachers they employ.

Among the many teachers I have supervised and trained were
certified mathematics teachers with at least a master's degree in

mathematics, or mathematics education, with content knowledge far beyond high-school-level mathematics. Like all New York City mathematics teachers, I had to take a Board of Education–designed test to be certified to teach in the New York City School System. In order to become a certified mathematics supervisor and teacher trainer, I had to take another rigorous three-part test. As a supervisor, part of my job description was teacher training, with emphasis on pedagogy. I have trained four mathematics teachers who had PhDs, the same qualification as Jason Zimba, the lead mathematics writer for the CCSS. They had advanced content knowledge far beyond and above what is required for certification to be a high school mathematics teacher. But that meant nothing if they did not master the pedagogical skills in the delivery of instruction to their students or if they had students who were lacking in the prerequisite knowledge for a particular class. Content knowledge in a subject at the level of university graduate is the necessary beginning qualification for a high school teacher.

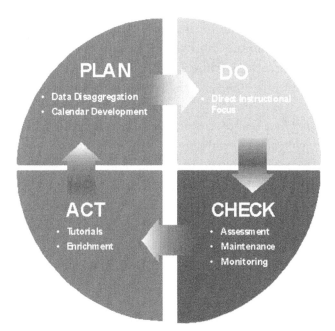

Figure 11.1: *Source: http://www.newcenturyeducation.org/ continuous-improvement/*

With this as minimum qualification, the most important aspect of teaching is mastery of pedagogical and classroom management skills that will enable the teacher to motivate and excite students through a passionate approach to the delivery of instruction. A teaching professional has an obligation to engage in what Dr. J. Edward Deming called "continuous improvement," as succinctly demonstrated in figure 11.1. I have been guided by that principle in my profession as a mathematics teacher, as a supervisor of mathematics teachers, and as a mathematics professor, and I have imparted the same to the teachers I have trained and supervised. This principle insists that no matter how accomplished a teacher believes that he or she is, there is always room for improvement.

In this endeavor, I applaud Exxon and their support for the National Math Science Initiative (NMSI). Teachers who are committed to continuous improvement will most certainly benefit from Exxon's support to improve the delivery of instruction in mathematics and science. The purpose of professional organizations such as the NTCM is to offer continuous improvement in teaching, through quarterly regional workshops and annual national and international conferences. On the matter of continuous improvement, here is a statement by perhaps the most famous high school mathematics teachers in the history of US education. Jaime Escalante, whose teaching story was featured in the movie *Stand and Deliver*, said the following:

> Since my first year of student teaching in Bolivia I have felt an obligation to make myself a better teacher and to profit from my mistakes. As an undergraduate I was closely watched, apprenticed and critiqued by an experienced teacher. Under his critical eye, I abandoned unworkable ideas and came to understand the importance of becoming much more communicative with the students and not simply working at the blackboard all day. This kind of practice teaching under a proven teacher is vital.[187]

For the record, the CCSS lead writer in mathematics, Jason Zimba, has a PhD in mathematical physics and therefore has a "deeper knowledge of the subject" than Jaime Escalante, the mathematics teachers in *Stand and Deliver*. Escalante had only a bachelor's degree in mathematics when he entered the teaching profession at Garfield High School, in Los Angeles. This is two levels below that of Jason Zimba. Escalante mastered pedagogy by the process of continuous improvement and gave a lot of his time to his students.[188] I could find no record of Jason Zimba having experience as a K–12 mathematics teacher or any formal education in pedagogy. If I had the option to choose between Zimba or Escalante to teach my own children, I would most certainly choose Escalante. The same choice would be made if I had the choice as a school district administrator to hire one or the other as a mathematics teacher.

No public high school would seek to hire teachers without basic content knowledge deep enough to teach mathematics at that level. Any school that admits only students meeting strict pre-admission criteria, while employing a set of certified teachers having mastery in pedagogy bolstered by continuous upgrading of teaching skills, will constitute one of the best schools anywhere in the world.

11.2 A Word about Teachers and Teacher Time

There are politicians who take pride in vilifying teachers and use them as scapegoats when educational outcomes are less than optimum. Some have said derisively that teachers are part-time workers. One twenty-first century presidential candidate campaigning in Pennsylvania said that there is nothing wrong with teachers having large class sizes. For such people, I would highly recommend seeing the movie *Stand and Deliver*. This movie tells the true story of one dedicated mathematics teacher, Jaime Escalante, who worked tirelessly with his students at home perhaps even more than at school. They will see that teaching is not just classroom time, but involves hours of working time beyond mandatory working hours. Escalante's students were not the gifted and well prepared, so he decided to start from ground zero with accelerated revision of the basics skills through long hours during the summer. His students did so well on the advanced placement calculus exam that the Educational Testing Service (ETS) concluded that all the students cheated. They had to repeat the test under ETS supervision.

Most of the students did better the second time around. The results reflected the dividends from investments in continuous pedagogical improvement supplemented by voluntary teacher time.

Take an average English or Social Studies teacher, with five classes averaging thirty students in each. The teacher gives a homework assignment to write a three-page essay. After collecting that essay, the teachers will have 450 pages to read and then return the results in a day or two. How does the teacher find school time to teach five classes and read the equivalent of a 450-page book? This work has to be done outside school time, mostly at home, taking hours, if the essay is to be checked for coherence, proper syntax, spelling, grammar, and other writing skills.

In the positions of supervisor of mathematics teachers in a high school, I have written commendation letters to teachers I've witnessed going far beyond the call of duty to provide the best education for their students. I've seen them coming to work hours before official school time to refine their preparation for the day's classes and staying after school for additional hours, to offer extra help to their students. These same teachers take home tests, quizzes, and special assignments to do the time-consuming work of marking and grading. I have also seen teachers spend their own money on educational materials that the school was unable to provide.

At the high school level, the mathematics teacher also teaches five classes per day, five days per week. These consist of an average of three different preparations, taken from the four-year high school mathematics curriculum. This means three different preparations each school day. Preparation time extends outside of school hours, especially for the less experienced teacher. It is mandatory that for each lesson, a teacher must have a well-structured written lesson plan containing specific objectives, a motivational activity, the development of the lesson, an application exercise for measuring the outcomes of the lesson, and a summary. It is a requirement that there must be a homework assignment for every mathematics lesson. This means homework must be assigned and checked daily. The effective mathematics teacher gives tests and quizzes in alternate weeks. If the average class size is thirty (and I've seen class sizes as high as forty students), the teacher with five classes will have an average of 150 students per day. If the teacher with five classes gives ten homework exercises per class, there will be three hundred homework exercises for each class. Multiplying this by five (each teacher has five classes) gives that teacher 1,500 items to check. This requires that the teacher must have a strategy to ascertain that every student did the assigned homework. Each time tests or quizzes are given, the teacher will have an average of 150 tests or 150 quizzes to mark and grade meticulously. Most teachers give special projects involving independent study and research for enrichment. At least 90 percent of the above obligations have to be done outside of school time. To state that teachers are part-time workers is not only disingenuous, but it is a specific disservice to the teaching profession. How about those congress-persons who work an average of only three days per week, with salaries and perquisites the average American will never see in a lifetime? After leaving congress, many become lobbyists earning millions of dollars to work against the public interest. Instead of making condescending statements about teachers, politicians would do well if each would ask the reflective question: what have I done since taking office to boost teacher morale in our country?

Let us stop the impulsive vilification of our teachers. Yes, like any other profession there is a small percent of bad apples. We have bad apple doctors, bad apple lawyers, bad apple CEOs of corporations, bad apple cops, bad apple clergymen, and a disproportionate set of bad apple congressional representatives, senators, and state governors. Indeed, there are bad apples in every category of work. Let us not paint all teachers with that same brush.

Ronald Reagan, as US president, was appreciative of teachers. He expressed profound respect for the profession when he said:

> *Every new year for the schoolteacher is like a new age of enlightenment in which young minds become awakened to the truths that we hold to be self-evident. You teach your students math and science and literature and expedient history—a variety of subjects. You give them many facts and much knowledge. But your task is greater than that because with the facts, you must impart the values that give them meaning and context—our most sacred values of human*

dignity and the worth of the individual.
In the hands of America's teachers rests the formidable
responsibility of molding and inspiring tomorrow's heroes —
the medical scientists who will invent cures for disease,
the businessmen who will found whole new industries,
the writers, artists, doctors — who knows, maybe even a
politician or two. [Laughter][189]

We are all products of teachers. Very few of us would be where we are today without intersecting with those who instruct us in classrooms.

Unionized sport figures are legally able to negotiate annual contracts in the multimillions of dollars per year, while some state governors find it expedient to eliminate collective bargaining rights for teachers. Teachers with PhDs in mathematics, physics, or chemistry will find it challenging, with rising inflation, to pay a mortgage, educate their children, and meet basic day-to-day expenses. Congressmen don't have to bargain for salary increases. They legislate themselves automatic salary increases every two years, even when there is no inflation. Now we have specious instruments, such as the unpiloted CCSS, with an evaluation component skewed to lower test scores, to influence low evaluation of teachers. With the public school closings due to negative evaluations, charter school entrepreneurs are waiting in the wings to hire these same teachers — but with pay cuts. In states like New Jersey and Wisconsin, governors take pride in cutting taxes while reducing pension benefits for teachers. Like any other set of workers, teachers need to feel appreciated.

If we really want to improve teacher quality, then we should consider incentives that would motivate qualified people to enter or stay in the profession. Rather than making teachers scapegoats and echoing past Undersecretary of Education Eugene Hickok's statement that "We need to get better teachers," why not propose positive initiatives designed to attract young people to the teaching profession? A great place to start is to ensure that salaries are fair and that pension benefits are guaranteed while giving teachers the tools to improve education. Accountability has its place, and no teacher should be exempt. But flawed teacher evaluation standards and cynical comments about teachers do nothing to improve the education of the nation's children.

11.3 Helping Teachers to Make the United States First in the World in Mathematics and Science

All great teachers know the importance of walking into a classroom with high expectations of their students. But they also know that students succeed best when they have the appropriate prerequisite knowledge and live in an environment that fosters such knowledge. This is the whole point of this letter. The US Customary System, now in current use across the country, is specifically regressive, in that it impedes rather than enhances learning the concepts for early introduction to algebra and other areas of mathematics and the sciences. The metric system does the opposite in that it is an enhancer for mathematics and a boost for science education. Most if not all scientific measurements are in metric units. This is where parental and taxpayer responsibility is paramount. They must get involved, particularly when the government behaves in unenlightened ways. If parents would let their congressional representatives know that they are in favor of phasing in the metric system in this country, it would get done. This is neither a Republican nor a Democratic issue. It is an education issue that should be of concern to all Americans.

It was Archimedes who said, "Give me a place to stand on, and I will move the world." He was talking about levers and leverage. Before we talk about getting "more qualified math teachers" and resort to explicit or implicit blame on school districts and try to modify teacher evaluation through "failure by design" conspiratorial protocols, we must be mindful that the teachers of today are products of yesterday's educational systems. The teachers of tomorrow will be the product of today's educational systems. If we want our students to compete on the same level as their international counterparts, we must provide the same level playing field for both teachers and students. Let us give our teachers a "place to stand on" by eliminating the measurement systems that impede and replace them with those that enhance learning. Let's stop the arbitrary imposition of standards by people whose prime purpose is their own self-interest and who have distorted ideas about how education works.

The American landing on the moon in 1969 was a triumph of American technology but not American ingenuity. The rocket-propulsion technology that enabled that monumental achievement was due to the scientific acumen of the German rocket scientist Wernher Von Braun.[190] The ubiquitous jet engine, now used to power the aircraft flights all over the world, was invented by the German scientist Dr. Franz Von Ohain and Sir Frank Whittle of England. A glance at the metric chart in figure 2 in chapter 2 will show that Germany changed to the metric system in 1872. Subsequently, the list of great German scientists, including Albert Einstein, Werner Heisenberg, Max Born, Max Planck, Hans Bethe, and Ervin Schroedinger, to name only a few, is a dazzling display of how an environment with the metric system can produce extraordinary scientists and mathematicians. Had the suggestion of President George Washington been heeded in 1790, the United States would be first on the list in figure 2., in chapter 2, and we may have been able to match the German achievements in mathematics and science.

Time is of the essence. The next generation of American children deserves an enriching learning environment of the kind that nurtured the likes of Wernher von Braun or Franz von Ohain and one that is commensurate with the money being spent per student. It will take ten years for the current five-year-old student to be qualified to take the PISA test at age fifteen. If we want our current five-year-olds to be ready in ten years when they are fifteen, we must remind our politicians that it was an act of an enlightened US Congress in 1968, three years after Great Britain adopted the metric system, that produced the report entitled "A Metric America: A Decision Whose Time has Come." Indeed, we are still waiting for that time to come, to actualize George Washington's eighteenth-century proposal, a time to end the under-education of America's children.

We are still a relatively young nation. As Americans we must make one of two choices. We can continue with the archaic US Customary Units of measurements, along with the useless Fahrenheit scale, and allow the cancer of the Common Core State Standards to metastasize; and in doing so, we will perpetuate the status quo of hazards that inhibit student learning in science and mathematics. Alternatively, we can choose to join the international community in adopting the metric system along with the Celsius scale and level the playing field for all our students. Instead of utilizing the CCSS, the product of David Coleman's Students Achievement Partners, let us engage the NTCM's Process Standards for Mathematics as a framework to construct modifications consistent with a metric system environment. In the restructuring process, let us pilot the idea of lowering the four basic operations of signed numbers into the elementary school curriculum, with the goal of starting algebra much earlier than is the current practice. Textbook publishers and software companies would be ready to provide the products needed for the new K–12 paradigm shift. Our teachers will respond with enthusiasm and verve, by nurturing and preparing more American students to excel as scientists, mathematicians, and engineers in our universities. As Americans, we will take pride in the byproduct of getting respectable placements in international competitions, as reflective of our country being a powerhouse in precollege preparation.

It is my belief, based on analysis, that if we choose the latter course of action, if the United States is added to the list of countries using the metric system, this country will add one more accolade to an impressive list of being the best in many aspects, particularly in technology. It is easy to envisage that in the future, the United States of America will reflect on this paradigm shift as the defining moment when we were able the begin the climb to attain and maintain an even higher level of supremacy in the world in mathematics and science education, as well as in engineering technology.

Yours sincerely,

Dillon M. Lobban, EdD

Mathematics Professor (Retired)

PART V

POSTSCRIPTS FOR HOME-SCHOOL PARENTS AND K-12 TEACHERS

Postscripts:
(P.S.1 - P.S.9)

Additional Enrichment for use by Parents and K–12 Teachers

In the introduction, I made the point that every parent has homeschooling responsibilities, in that there is full-time as well as part-time homeschooling, and the parameters of each category were explained.

Since this book is a letter to parents as well as educators, I'm using the device of postscript (PS) to append the next nine activities and suggestions for exploration and enhancement. Not only home-school parents but elementary school teachers will find them very exciting as tools for mathematics enrichment. I have personally used some of them in workshops for mathematics teachers and the feedback is that they have found them informative as well as effective tools for the teaching-learning process.

P.S. 1: Explanation of Inequality Symbols

In discussing how to write numbers in scientific notation of the form $a \times 10^n$, I introduced the notion of an inequality by stating that the number **a** must satisfy the statement $1 \leq a < 10$, which means that **a** must be a number that is greater than or equal to 1 and less than ten. The following is the explanation I promised.

One of the beautiful aspects of mathematics is that we can succinctly write verbal statements in symbolic form. In the chart in figure PS 1.1, the two numbers 3 and 8 are selected. The chart shows all possible symbols of inequality that can be expressed as relations between 3 and 8.

Symbols of Inequality

If two numbers are not equal, the relationship between them can be expressed in several different ways.

Symbol	Example	Read
>	8 > 3	8 is greater than 3
<	3 < 8	3 is less than 8
≯	3 ≯ 8	3 is not greater than 8
≮	8 ≮ 3	8 is not less than 3
≥	8 ≥ 3	8 is greater than or equal to 3
≤	3 ≤ 8	3 is less than or equal to 8
≠	8 ≠ 3	8 is not equal to 3

Figure PS 1.1: *Source: Dressler, Keenan, Gantert, and Occhiogrosso. Integrated Mathematics, Second Edition ed. Vol. Course I. New York, New York: Amsco School Publications, 1989. 26.*

We'll take this further in figure PS 1.2, where both negative and positive numbers are involved.

The first two lines in PS1.2 are specific cases stating that if a number **a** is strictly less than a number **b**, then this can be written as **a < b**. If a number **a** is strictly greater than a number **b**, then this can be written as **a > b**.

Lines 3, 4, and 5 have to do with the logic of the word "or." For example, in line 3, the statement $-8 \leq 10$ is a disjunction of two statements. These statements are: "−8 is less than 10" OR "−8 is equal to 10." In logic, a disjunction is true if only one of the statements is true. For example, take the case where a child named Mary is in her room. The statement: "Mary is sleeping or Mary is awake" is a true statement even though one of the statements that form the disjunction must be false.

No.	Inequality	Verbal Equivalent
1	$6 < 10$	6 is less than 10
2	$9 > -5$	9 is greater than -5
3	$-8 \leq 10$	-8 is less than or equal to 10
4	$10 \geq -8$	10 is greater than or equal to -8
5	$6 \leq 6$	6 is less than or equal to 6
6	$6 \geq 6$	6 is greater than or equal to 6
7	$-3 < 4 < 9$	4 is less than 9 and greater than -3
8	$1 \leq a < 10$	The variable a is less than 10 and greater than or equal to 1

Figure PS 1.2

Mary cannot both be asleep and awake at the same time. This demonstrates why a disjunction is true if only one of the statements is true. In the next two lines we have $6 \leq 6$ and $6 \geq 6$, which are both true statements, resulting in the mathematical conclusion is that $6 = 6$. It is a mathematical proposition that **if two numbers a and b are such that a ≤ b and a ≥ b, then a = b.**

Now that we understand the symbols of inequality, we can state a very important mathematical property. **If two numbers x and y are chosen from the number line, then one and only one of the following statements is true.**

$$x < y, x = y, x > y$$

P.S. 2: Helping your Child Learn Addition and Multiplication Facts.

In chapter 6, the tables for addition and multiplication facts were presented, and I promised to give some hints as to how your child could study and memorize the elements of each set of facts. Please bear in mind that learning styles vary between children. What prompts learning in one child may not work for another. I will suggest some tools that work for most children when studying mathematics. Observing patterns works for most if not all children. We assume that most parents will teach their children how to count as early as possible. On that point, here is a useful suggestion by developmental psychologist Judith Hudson:

> *You can introduce the idea of numbers when your child is as young as 12 months by counting small sets of items — "How many buttons? One, two!" — and singing songs and rhymes that include counting, such as "One, two, buckle my shoe," "Five little pumpkins sitting on a fence," and so on. When your child is 2 years old, she may learn to count up to 10 by rote, though she won't really understand the concept of counting objects yet, and may skip around in her counting — "One, two, five, six..." Don't worry about her mistakes in counting — the fact that she's reciting numbers means she's learning the correct names. Next she'll learn to point to objects and label them with numbers (even if they're not the correct ones). Take advantage of everyday opportunities to count together; setting the table is a good example. "One napkin for mommy, one napkin for daddy, one for you! One, two, three napkins!" At first your child may say there are three napkins no matter how many you've actually laid out, but at some point she'll start to understand that the word "three" stands for the number of napkins.[191]*

As soon as they have mastered counting from 1 to 100, have them count by twos, by fives, certainly by tens and even backward, for example, from 10 backward to 0 or 30 backward to 20.

It would be useful to get a copy of the elementary school curriculum and use the Internet for help and reinforcement. Specifically, go to www.youtube.com and type the concept in the search engine. The algorithms will prioritize what you are searching for if you phrase the search beginning with "How to." For example "How to learn addition facts." As suggested before, you should be selective, because there are several presentations of the same concept, and, as you will observe, some presentations have more clarity than others.

The tables containing addition and multiplication facts are filled with patterns. Patterns can provide the basis for structured memorization and are very powerful for discovery in mathematics. You may observe these patterns, or better still, get them from the Internet, but let your children discover them for themselves. After having them discover as many as they can, you may point out those that are missed by asking questions that prompt analytic observation.

In the chart on addition facts it would be productive to ask your youngster to list, by writing, all the numbers that add up to the number 10. You may want to state that "sum means to add." And then, have your youngster write down the pairs of numbers whose sum is 10 or 11, or 12, and so on. Ask the question: What is the result when 10 is added to a single-digit number? You will expect them to state that the answer replaces zero with the number. For example $10 + 8 = 18$. These are only a few of the many concepts that can be discovered with the long-term result that your child is fluent with the basic addition facts.

If you observe that your youngster needs help, use well-structured questions to lead them to the discovery. Avoid the urge to "show" your child everything. Prompt them to think critically through well-placed questions such as, "What patterns do you observe in the addition facts chart?" Studies have shown that when children discover concepts on their own, learning by retention is more indelible than when they are shown the concepts by parents or teachers. Earlier in section 5.4 the "Socratic Method" was mentioned. Teaching by questioning originated with the great Greek philosopher Socrates, who, it is said, taught critical thinking merely by asking the right questions. That is why this way of teaching is called the **Socratic Method**. The operative methodology is called "constructivism." In this kind of instruction, students learn by thinking critically and by "constructing" their own understanding of key concepts. For example, most students know the multiplication table by memorization. But we can use a product statement such as $3 \times 4 = 12$ to ask a number of questions to ensure understanding.

To do this, teachers use the Ask → Elicit paradigm. The teacher's lesson plan would contain the questions to be "asked" and the answers he/she expects to "elicit" from the students. Students should be instructed to give full statement answers and to avoid one-word answers. The other side of this advice is to avoid questions that give a "yes" or "no" answer simply because these words give no indication of definitive comprehension.

Let's get back to example in the product statement $3 \times 4 = 12$.

Ask: Which number is the multiplier?
Elicit: The multiplier is 3

Ask: Which number is the multiplicand?
Elicit: The multiplicand is 4.

Ask: When two numbers are multiplied, what is the name of the answer?
Elicit: When two numbers are multiplied, the answer is called the product.

Ask: Why is $3 \times 4 = 12$ a true statement?
Elicit: Because multiplication is addition of the multiplicand the number of times indicated by the multiplier. An alternative and acceptable answer could be that multiplication is a shortcut for adding the same number a multiple of times. Hence $3 \times 4 = 4 + 4 + 4 = 12$.

The point can be driven home by discussing the same approach with the commutative equivalent of 3×4, which is 4×3.

Using the same Ask → Elicit paradigm, we would be able to elicit that $4 \times 3 = 3 + 3 + 3 + 3 = 12$. The **commutative** property is very important for algebra and later courses in mathematics.

As regards the multiplication facts on the "Multiplication Table Chart," do a search titled "Patterns of multiplication facts" at "www.youtube.com."

I would suggest that you have your youngster write a separate multiplication table chart for each number on 3×5 cards. They can carry these cards in their pockets and study them as the last activity before going to sleep and first after waking up. They can even review while using the bathroom. The process will allow recognition of the easy ones such as the 2 times table, the 5 times table, the 10 times table, and the 11 times table. Also, the act of writing will reinforce the learning process. Avoid any form of coercion but consider giving a meaningful reward when each time table is mastered.

Do not take the advice of some educators that memorization of times tables is not essential. Memorization has its place, in learning the vocabulary of a foreign language, symbols in chemistry, and certainly in learning multiplication tables.

I will illustrate one of the most interesting of the times tables, by making a multiplication table chart of the number 9 from 9×1 to 9×10. See figure PS 2.1. I've left out $9 \times 11 = 99$ because this is the same as 11×9 from the multiplication table for 11. As for $9 \times 12 = 108$, your youngster can study this separately, but it is left out of the table for a reason, which will be apparent.

9×1	9
9×2	18
9×3	27
9×4	36
9×5	45
9×6	54
9×7	63
9×8	72
9×9	81
9×10	90

Figure PS 2.1: *The Nine Times Table*

I would suggest that, before reading further, you should peruse the table and look for as many patterns as possible. After searching, did you discover the following interesting details about the 9 times table.

1. The sum of the digits of each product is 9.
   For example: $9 \times 2 = 18$ and $1 + 8 = 9$, $9 \times 3 = 27$ and $2 + 7 = 9$,
   and so on down to $9 \times 10 = 90$ and $9 + 0 = 9$.

2. For the next interesting pattern in the 9 times table, there is no loss of value if I change the product $9 \times 1 = 9$ to $9 \times 1 = 09$, since 9 is equivalent to 09.

Your child may discover that counting down the tens column, we have 0,1,2,3,4,5,6,7,8,9 and the ones column reverses the process counting 9,8,7,6,5,4,3,2,1,0.

9×1	09
9×2	18
9×3	27
9×4	36
9×5	45
9×6	54
9×7	63
9×8	72
9×9	81
9×10	90

Figure PS 2.2

3. Another pattern item is that if the first product, which is 09, is turned around, we get the last product in the chart, which is 90. Continuing this turnaround process, 18 turned around becomes 81, 27, becomes 72, 36 becomes 63, and 45 becomes 54.

4. There is one more pattern that can be useful. Let's say you are in a remote area without a cell phone, a computer, or any calculation device and you cannot recall the product 9×7. How could we determine the answer from the patterns we've observed in the 9 times table? Note that each product obtained from nine times a number begins with 1 less than the number being multiplied by 9. For example, $9 \times 4 = 36$. the "3" in 36 is 1 less than 4. In other words $3 = 4 - 1$. Note that this pattern holds throughout the 9 times table. Now let's get back to 9×7. We'll use two observed patterns. First the answer begins with $7 - 1 = 6$ and since the sum of the two digits is always 9. Then 9×7 must be 63 because $6 + 3 = 9$.

You can see my demonstration of the above by typing "Dillon Lobban—Nine times table patterns" at www.youtube.com.

Mastering the addition and multiplication facts in a metric and Celsius culture will provide them with tools for early introduction to algebra, satisfying the NMAP primary objective, i.e., to "focus on preparing students to take and succeed in algebra."[192]

P.S. 3: How the Game of Golf Facilitates Algebraic Concepts

Encourage your children to get acquainted with the game of golf. It is the only game in American sports in which your child will directly encounter both negative and positive numbers. There is a great program called "The First Tee" (see www.firsttee.org) which is involved with teaching the game and its sterling ethical principles to school-age children. You may even want to suggest, at the next parent-teacher meeting, that the school district get affiliated with the program. Acquaintance with golf comes with a magnificent behavioral dividend, because the game is known for its exceptional ethical characteristics such as insisting on personal honesty, courtesy, and respect for others as well as fostering honor and integrity. It is the only game I can think of in which players call a penalty on themselves or even disqualify themselves, when no one but the player sees an infraction of the rules. The late Arnold Palmer, called the "King of Golf," was a trustee of The First Tee organization proclaimed that children learning golf also gain "important values, like doing the right thing, even when no one is watching."[193] Rickie Fowler, a young professional golfer with great potential, is involved with The First Tee. He made the following comments about the organization:

> It exposes young people to the game that promotes values like honesty, responsibility, and judgment; values that can guide them for the rest of their lives. The First Tee gives young people room to grow and along the way have a little fun.[194]

The mathematical dividend is that it exposes young children to signed numbers. Golfers' scores are negative if they are playing under par and positive if they are playing over par. A look at the scoreboard of the average game of golf will show that the leader is the player with the highest negative score. For example, if you and your child watched the 2014 Hero Golf Challenge tournament on NBC Sports TV, a golf match designed to raise funds for the Tiger Wood's Foundation, you would have seen that twenty-one–year-old Jordan Spieth won with a record score of –26. The runner-up in second place was Henrik Stenson, with a score of –16.

Children do not have to play the game, although that would be excellent, but with the Golf Channel on cable TV, which is devoted solely to golf, they can watch and learn the game on television. If you are able to take them to the golf course and watch the scoreboard, it will be a tremendous educational experience for some simple problems in signed number operations and for beginning algebra.

With knowledge of how the game of golf is scored, a child in the third, fourth, or fifth grade should be able to solve the following four problems that are taken from a ninth-grade textbook in beginning algebra.

Add the following pairs of signed numbers:

1. $(+3) + (+7)$
2. $(-5) + (-3)$
3. $(-8) + (+5)$
4. $(-5) + (+5)$

The game is played with 18 holes, with each hole defined by a tee-to-green **par** number. There are par 3, par 4, and par 5 holes. On a par 4 hole, for example, if a player takes 4 shots to get the ball into the hole from tee to green, he has a par or even score on that hole. If the player takes 3 shots to get the ball into the hole, he has a score of one under par. This is called a "birdie" and the official score is –1 for that par 4 hole. If the player takes 5 shots to get the ball in the hole, he has a bogey and the score is recorded as +1.

On the golf leader board with regular scoring, a player gets –1 for a birdie, –2, for an eagle, –3 for double eagle or "albatross," +1 for a bogey, +2 for a double bogey, +3 for a triple bogey, and so on, and, as stated before, par for an even (E) score. In a regular golf tournament, the leader board shows the cumulative score of each player at any given time during play.

The following four hypothetical game scores, respectively associated with problems No. 1 through No. 4, will demonstrate how the scoring in golf can be very powerful for learning signed number operations.

In Problem No. 1, (+3) + (+7), a golfer on an eighteen-hole golf course had 3 bogies or +3 on the front nine holes, and also made 7 bogies or +7 on the back nine. At the end of the round, the total score would be the sum (+3) + (+7) to get a score of +10 on the leader board and is said to be "ten over par." This would be a bad day for the golfer, but is an example of adding **two positive numbers**.

In Problem No. 2, (−5) + (−3), another golfer (maybe your child's favorite in the game) on the same course had 5 birdies or −5 on the front nine holes, and another 3 birdies or −3 on the back nine. At the end of the round, the total score would be the sum (−5) + (−3) to get a score of −8 or "eight under par." This is an example of **adding two negative numbers**.

In Problem No. 3, (−8) + (+5), a golfer in one round made 8 birdies or −8, but ran into trouble on another round and made 5 bogies or +5. The score at the end of two rounds would be the (−8) + (+5), resulting in a score of −3. In this example, your child will be **adding two numbers with unlike signs**.

In Problem No. 4, (−5) + (+5), the golfer had 5 birdies and closed out the round with a score of −5. The next day he was not as sharp, and scores 5 bogies or + 5. After two rounds he is now at even par or "E," because (−5) + (+5) = 0.

In the last example, your child will experience adding numbers that are mathematical opposites. The easy concept of **opposite of a number** is fundamental for algebra. The **opposite** of a number is its counterpart (the same distance from zero) on the opposite side of zero on the number line as illustrated in figure PS 3.1 Here we see that the opposite of 5 is −5. Conversely, the opposite of −5 is 5.

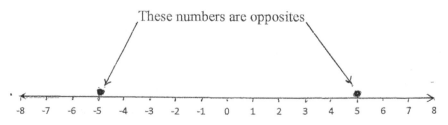

These numbers are opposites

Figure PS 3.1: *Source: http://www.freelearningchannel.com*

This brings us to the proposition involving the opposite of a number. It states the following:

If two numbers are opposites, then their sum is zero.

Conversely: **If the sum of two numbers is zero, then each number is the opposite of the other.**

An algebra textbook will explain that a minus sign next to the left of an algebraic expression, in parenthesis, means the **opposite of** the expression inside the parenthesis. For example the expression −(+5) can be read as the opposite of +5, which is −5. In shortened form we would write −(+5) = −5. Similarly −(−5) = +5. In general, if x is any number, then **−(−x) = +x**, as can be seen in any textbook on beginning algebra. This translates into the concept that **a negative of a negative is a positive**.

Speaking of algebra, the addition problems discussed here make it easy to add algebraic expressions. For example if a child can add (+3) + (+5) to get +8, he or she can add variable expressions such as 3b + 5b to get 8b. This is the same as adding 3 balls + 5 balls to get 8 balls. If the child can add (−8) + (+5), then he or she can add −8x + 5x to get an answer of −3x.

The rules for addition of signed numbers will be easy to grasp when the lessons are formally taught in a classroom, but the child who is familiar with the scoring in golf will have a tremendous head start in a class with children who may be encountering negative and positive numbers for the first time in the sixth grade. In fact, in a school that has accelerated programs, your child would be recognized and placed on track accordingly. Having your child learn and watch the game of golf will bring your child to the point where there is "More focus on positive and negative numbers."

Incidentally, professional golfer Phil Mickelson, working together with ExxonMobil, has created the Mickelson-ExxonMobil Teachers Academy, whose mission is as follows:

To conduct a professional development academy for teachers of grades 3–5 that results in improved learning experiences for their students by:

- *enhancing grade-appropriate mathematics and science content knowledge;*

- *demonstrating the interrelationships between scientific inquiry and mathematical problem solving;*

- *using the tools of mathematics to build understanding and connections to science concepts; and*

- *modeling "best practices" in teaching and learning.*[195]

Parents can make a great impression at their school by recommending their grade 3–5 teachers to the Academy for developmental workshops. See the details at http://www.sendmyteacher.com/.

P.S. 4: Using Two-Color Counters for Adding and Subtracting Integers

In chapter 5, we read that the Canadian mathematics curriculum suggests the use of "two-colour counters" to explore operations with positive and negative numbers. (Note that the word "colour" in Canada is the same as "color" in the US.)

Before engaging in the exercises, you'll need to get a set two-color counters, as in figure P.S.4.1, where each chip has a red side and a yellow side. In the diagrams below, the yellow side appears light gray and the red side appears dark gray (almost black). I will use the words "yellow and "red" in explaining each exercise.

Figure P.S. 4.1: *Source: http://www.amazon.com/Learning-Resources-Two-Color-Counters-Manipulatives/dp/B0017D9BDG*

I have used two-color counters in classrooms and in teacher workshops. This manipulative is very effective in reinforcing addition and subtraction of integers. Teachers who had never used them before were awed by them as a teaching tool for adding and subtracting of negative and positive numbers. They are very effective for students working in groups. As a parent, you can invite your child's classmates over for the exercises I'll be demonstrating below.

The key to understanding how two-color counters work is the concept of "value." I will take you through a set of exercises that you can experience and practice by yourself, and subsequently with your child at home. Don't be surprised if your child's teacher is not familiar with two-color counters. Your child could make a great impression in "show and tell" if his or her teacher has never experienced color counters before.

In these exercises we'll use the counters to represent integers. We will use one color to represent a positive integer and the other to represent a negative integer.

Here, we'll use one "yellow" counter to represent a positive integer, and a "red" counter to represent a negative integer. So, one yellow counter has the value of +1, and one red counter has the value of -1.

As stated before, the notion of "**value**," is very important. For example the following groupings have respective **values** of +5, -2, and -3.

When using two-color counters, it is very important to be able to determine the **zero value**. The following groupings all have the value of zero. That's because there are an equal number of red and yellow counters in each group. You may recall that we previously determined that when two numbers are opposites, their sum is zero.

Using two-color counters as concrete objects that children may touch renders abstract mathematical concepts more understandable. Modeling addition and subtraction in such a way greatly assists children in learning these operations for beginning algebra. The University of Illinois Extension in an article entitled "Learning Styles" made the following instructive statement: "Most children show a preference for one of the following basic learning styles: visual, auditory, kinesthetic/ manipulative."[196] The article went on to state that:

> *Trying different methods of learning may prevent the*
> *children from feeling frustrated and inadequate when they*
> *are not able to work up to their potential. Experimenting*

with different learning styles and environments may improve the child's accomplishments and feelings of achievement.[197]

Children can start using these color-counter manipulative, sometimes called "color chips," in the lower grades, thus giving them an intuitive head start in algebra. As for the rules of the operations, children can learn them in a constructivist manner through raw intuition and pattern observation. Constructivism in teaching is the process by which children are encouraged to discover concepts for and by themselves or, in other words, construct their own learning.

We are now ready to perform the operations of addition and subtraction of integers using two-color counters. First we will need a "workplace." At school, this workplace is the student's desk, or table if there is a math lab. At home it can be a table or any horizontal surface.

Let's be clear on what we mean by addition and subtraction.

1. Addition means adding color counters to the workplace.

2. Subtraction means removing color counters from the workplace.

I will use one or more rectangles marked as the "workplace." The rectangle marked "final value of the workplace" will contain the answer.

Let's begin with addition of integers.

Example #1. Add (-3) + (-2)

Begin by placing three red counters in the workplace. After (-2) is added to the workplace we get the result below. The final value (the answer) is -5.

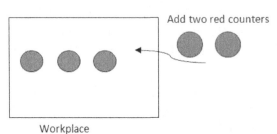

Add two red counters

Workplace

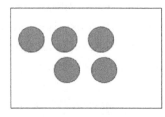

Final value in the Workplace

Example #2. Add (+4) + (-3)

Add four yellow chips to the workplace to represent +4, and then add three red chips to represent -3.

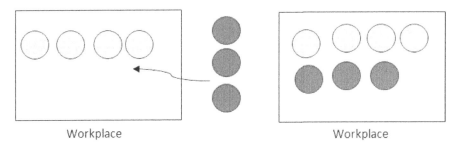

Workplace   Workplace

The three zero pairs make the value of the workplace +1. Therefore, the answer is +1.

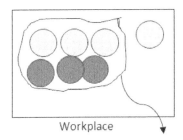

Workplace

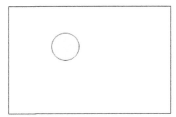

Final Value of the workplace

We will now model the operation of subtraction.

Example #3. Subtract (-5) - (-3)

Recall that subtraction means to remove color counters from the workplace. So in this subtraction example we must remove three red counters. After removing them, two are left, so the answer is -2.

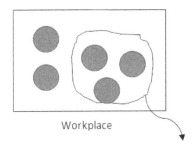

Workplace

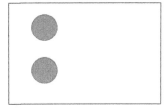

Final Value of the Workplace

The next subtraction example demonstrates the infectious beauty of mathematics. Here we go!

Example #4. Subtract (-2) - (+3)

Here's the challenge. If subtraction means to remove color counters, then to subtract +3 means we have to remove three yellow chips from the workplace. Since there are no yellow chips, how are we going to do that? Well here is mathematics at its most beautiful. The zero value will come to the rescue!

We'll keep the value of −2 in the workplace by adding sufficient zero pairs. In this case we add three zero pairs, and the workplace changes to the rectangle on the right. Note the workplace still has a value of −2. Mathematically, $-2 + 0 + 0 + 0 = -2$.

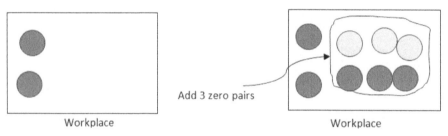

Now we can remove (subtract) +3, therefore the answer is -5.

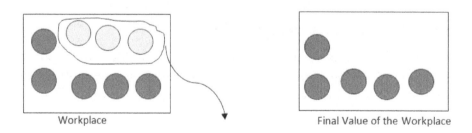

Magical, isn't it?

An accompanying exercise booklet comes with each package of two-color counters. You can have lots of fun with this, and your child will have a tremendous head start in class. If you are doing homeschooling, it is absolutely essential to get these two-color counters.

The next postscript (P.S.5) will be about two simple but important key concepts for beginning algebra and can be found in any algebra textbook.

P.S. 5: Get Acquainted with the Opposite and the Absolute Value of a Number

We have previously discussed the **opposite of a number**, in postscript P.S. 3, as an important concept. (As a reminder, pairs of numbers, such as 6 and +6, are opposites of each other.) Another concept that is necessary for beginning algebra is the concept of the **absolute value of a number**. This is an easy concept to understand. The absolute value of a number can be obtained by stripping away the sign attached to the number. Hence, the absolute value of +6 is 6. Likewise, the absolute value of −6 is also 6. If the number has no sign attached, the absolute value is the number itself. The definition comes from the idea that absolute value is a measure of distance, and in mathematics distance is always positive. The absolute value represents the distance of a signed number when counting from zero on the number line. The distance is obtained by counting the spaces between zero and the point labeled as the signed number. For example, with the number −7, counting from zero gives us 7 spaces, and thus the absolute value of −7 is 7. The same procedure holds for +7.

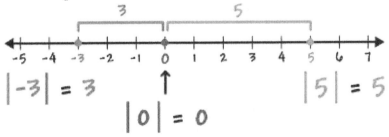

Figure PS. 5.1: *Source: www.coolmath.com*

Part of the beauty and elegance that adds to the joy of mathematics is that a verbal phrase or statement can be expressed in simple symbolic form. For example, the notation for the absolute value a variable number x is written $|x|$. Hence, the statement "The absolute value of −6 is 6" can be succinctly written symbolically as, $|-6| = 6$. In like manner, "The absolute value of +6 is 6" becomes $|+6| = 6$. When the number is positive, some teachers will leave out the positive sign, and this is acceptable. In other words, $|+6| = 6$ could be written $|6| = 6$.

See figure PS 5.1, for a geometric explanation of the absolute values of three numbers, −3, 5 or +5, and 0.

As soon as students have knowledge of negative and positive numbers, the concept of the opposite of a number, and the absolute value of a number, they are ready to go beyond intuition to the formal algorithms of the four basic operations (addition, subtraction, multiplication, and division) of signed numbers. This sets the average student on a direct and easy path to algebra and to master the simple tools to solve problems in discrete and continuous mathematics.

In this section we discussed only addition and subtraction of integers. This is because this particular manipulative easily lends itself well to these two operations. Two-color counters can also be used to demonstrate multiplication and division of signed numbers. For this I would suggest that you go to www.youtube.com and type in "how to use two-color counters in multiplication and division."

In section 10.4, we observed that in the addition of two signed numbers there were two patterns, one for adding numbers with the same sign and the other for adding numbers with unlike signs. Now that we understand the meaning of absolute value and the opposite of a number, we can restate the observed patterns as formal algebraic propositions.

Propositions for the addition of signed numbers:

1. When adding two numbers with like signs, add the absolute values of the numbers and keep the sign of the numbers being added.
2. When adding two numbers with unlike signs, subtract the smaller absolute value from the larger absolute value. The answer will take the sign of the number with the larger absolute value. For example: Add (−8) + (+3)

We proceed as follows: $|-8| = 8$, and $|+3| = 3$. And so, $8 - 3 = 5$. Since the number with the larger absolute is -8, the answer 5, will take the sign of -8, to become -5. Thus $(-8) + (+3) = -5$.

Since we now understand the opposite of a number, we can now formally state the singular proposition for subtraction of signed numbers in one statement as follows:

Subtraction Proposition: *To subtract two numbers taken in order, add the opposite of the second number to the first number, as in the scheme below.*

Note that this proposition transforms subtraction into an addition problem. That is the reason we must understand addition of signed numbers before we can understand subtraction.

For example, in elementary school arithmetic, we know that in regular arithmetic, $6 - 4$ is 2. This simple whole-number exercise can be expressed as a signed number problem as follows: $6 - 4 = (+6) - (+4)$. Applying the subtraction proposition: we get the addition problem $(+6) + (-4)$, and the answer is 2.

Here's an interesting subtraction problem: $0 - (-6)$. Using the proposition, this problem becomes $0 + (+6) = 6$.

You will not get a firm grasp of the concepts from merely reading the above presentations. A textbook on signed numbers will have extensive explanations and examples, along with several exercises. Practicing these exercises is absolutely essential to get a solid grasp of the concepts. That is why every mathematics lesson must be augmented by homework, and every mathematics textbook has multiple sets of exercises for each concept.

P.S. 6: Using Pattern Blocks for Geometry, Fractions, and Other Areas of Mathematics

Manipulatives are very powerful tools for hands-on practice, and more importantly the learning process for understanding fractions as well as geometry, algebra, and even science. For geometry and fractions I would suggest getting a set of pattern blocks. See figure PS 6.1.

Pattern blocks are excellent in giving students hands-on learning experiences in geometry. A package such as the one seen in figure PS 6.1 contains geometric shapes such hexagons, trapezoids, equilateral triangles, and rhombuses. Students can get the geometric "angle sense" of particular angle measurements. They can compare the angles of a regular hexagon, whose measures are 120 degrees, and observe that such angles are twice the angles of an equilateral triangle, whose measure are 60 degrees. Knowledge of angular geometry is the first step toward studying trigonometry and then on to calculus in later grades in high school.

Pattern blocks are indispensible in helping children through hands-on activities to learn the concepts underlying the definition of a fraction and basic operations with fractions. I will not attempt to give examples here. You can learn a lot more about how to use pattern blocks on www.youtube.com. For lessons on fractions, for example, type into the YouTube search engine, "How to use pattern blocks to add fractions." You will see that there are lots of enrichment activities to choose from.

Figure PS 6.1: *Source: http://keenonkindergarten.blogspot.com/2012_09_01_archive.html*

P.S. 7: Home—School Experiment—Verifying the Equation of a Pendulum

I had mentioned that the irrational number pi is included in the equation of the pendulum of your clock. If you have visited the United Nations building in New York City, you have seen a very large pendulum in operation. The motion of the pendulum contains several qualities that are representative of scientific phenomena in the universe. It facilitates the study of motion, velocity, gravity, and energy, both potential and kinetic.

You could get your youngster engaged in a very simple but very interesting and informative science activity with a pendulum. Since the pendulum is attached to a fixed point, each swing of the pendulum bob traces out an arc or part of a circle whose radius is the connecting string between the bob and the fixed point. See figure PS 7.1.

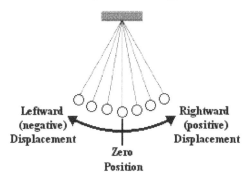

Figure PS7.1: *Source: http://www.physicsclassroom.com/class/waves/Lesson-0/Pendulum-Motion.*

Since a circle is involved, it should not be surprising that the equation of a pendulum, involves the number pi or π. That equation of the pendulum is as follows:

$$T = 2\pi \sqrt{\frac{L}{g}}$$

The letter **T** is called the period, the time required to complete a full cycle; **L** is the length of the string and **g** is the gravitational constant.

You can test the validity of this equation with your youngsters by helping or having them make a pendulum, using a plumb bob (you can get one at most hardware stores) and a string.

Start the observation by making the pendulum swing from a given height with the string very short. Keep increasing the length of the string and record the time of the swing. You'll observe that as you lengthen the string, the swings become slower. The mathematical explanation for this is that there are only two variables in the equation, namely, the period **T**, and the length of the string L. The other quantities in the equation, 2, π, and g (the acceleration due to gravity), are all fixed, so scientists call them **constants**. Since the time, **T**, depends only on the length of the string, **L**, we would say in fancy mathematical language, "T is a function of L". This can be written **symbolically as T = f(L)**. The beauty of the equation is that the weight of the pendulum plays no part in the period, except that if the weight is too light, friction from air currents may cause interference. If the experiment is done in a vacuum, the weight of the pendulum would have zero effect.

P.S. 8: The Fibonacci Number Sequence

Beginning in the fourth grade and up, get your youngster acquainted with the Fibonacci sequence of numbers. The numbers in order are 0, 1, 1, 2, 3, 5, 8, 13, 21, 34, 55, 89, 144, … If the pattern is identified, your child will be able to list the next number and each successor in the sequence to as many places as possible. First, let your child try to discover the pattern through observation. If he or she gets stumped, ask the question: what is the relationship between each number and its two predecessors? The child should discover that each number is obtained by taking the sum of its two predecessors. For example 13 = 8 + 5, 21 = 13 + 8, 34 = 21 + 13 and so on. Your child should then be able to determine that the next number after 144 is 233, since 89 + 144 = 233. It's an effective way for elementary school children to practice addition of whole numbers through pattern observation. The Fibonacci numbers can be found in interesting places in nature. Counting the rows or number of "buttons" in a row of the average pineapple will result in a Fibonacci number. The same goes for the artichoke, the sunflower spirals, and the shell of the nautilus, among others. As the numbers in the sequence get larger, if you divide one number by its predecessor, you'll get the constant irrational number 1.618… This number is called the **Golden Ratio**, and is said to have been used in art and architecture from the time of the ancient Greeks. You can learn more about these numbers by reading the small booklet *Fascinating Fibonaccis* by Trudi Hammel Garland, or by simply doing an Internet search on Google, Yahoo, or YouTube.

P.S. 9: Patterns in Pascal's Triangle

Another fascinating set of numbers for your youngster's enrichment is the scheme of Pascal's triangle (See figure PS 9.1). It has many patterns for discovery and is related to the Fibonacci numbers. An Internet search on "Pascal's Triangle" can provide you with more exciting information on the applications and perspectives on the beauty of this set of numbers. You can make the triangle as big as you want by constructing the next line after the last. You may want to engage your youngster in this activity by trying to generate the next line in figure PS 9.1 by discovering the pattern, enabling each line to be derived from the one above. Your youngster may make discoveries that escaped your thinking! By generating new rows in Pascal's triangle, your child will be practicing addition of whole numbers. Furthermore, knowledge of this arrangement of numbers is great preparation for later mathematics such as intermediate algebra.

Rather than telling you more about this very interesting and useful set of numbers for higher-level mathematics, I will assign to you the task of researching "Pascal's Triangle" using Internet search engines. You can also get an enriching set of activities in a book entitled *Pascal's Triangle* by Thomas M. Green and Charles L. Hamberg. For further exploration, you can always get personal explanatory help from www.youtube.com. This is another opportunity to practice addition of whole numbers while offering young students a device that prepares them for intermediate algebra.

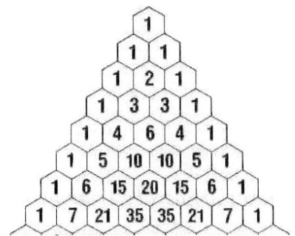

Figure PS 9.1, Pascal's Triangle: *Source: http://www.discreteteaching.com/documents/pascaler/PascalTalk.pdf*

Pascal's triangle is an important prerequisite for a very important concept in intermediate algebra, called the binomial theorem (see figure P S 9.2, below). When I encountered this expression for the first time, I was blown away by its beauty. I had looked ahead in my textbook and discovered that by the end of my course I would understand it, and I couldn't wait. I read ahead of my teacher and understood it before it was taught to me. This theorem is used in the study of statistics and probability, and is very useful for one of the early proofs in differential calculus.

What happens when you multiply a binomial by itself...many times?

Here is the answer:

$$(a + b)^n = \sum_{k=0}^{n} \binom{n}{k} a^{n-k} b^k$$

Don't worry...I will explain it all!

Figure PS 9.2: *Source: http://www.mathsisfun.com/algebra/binomial-theorem.html*

This can be found, as indicated, at the website www.mathisfun.com. As you can see, the person stating the formula is inviting you for an explanation at the website. Your youngster may not understand the binomial theorem before getting to intermediate algebra, but Pascal's triangle and the discovery of its many patterns can certainly be handled by third graders and up.

REFERENCES

[1] Harris, William. "Why Isn't the U.S. on the Metric System?" HowStuffWorks. Accessed July 21, 2015. http://science.howstuffworks.com/why-us-not-on-metric-system1.htm.

[2] Gerald R. Ford, "Statement on Signing the Metric Conversion Act of 1975." December 23, 1975. Online by Gerhard Peters and John T. Woolley, The American Presidency Project. Accessed July 21, 2015. http://www.presidency.ucsb.edu/ws/?pid=5454.

[3] Ibid.

[4] Exxon commercial "Lets Solve This." YouTube. Posted by Max Wx. Accessed 6/6/14. https://www.youtube.com/watch?v=cfGHDvBvI6g.

[5] Layton, Lindsey. "U.S. Students Lag around Average on International Science, Math and Reading Test." Washington Post. December 3, 2013. Accessed April 1, 2015. http://www.washingtonpost.com/local/education/us-students-lag-around-average-on-international-science-math-and-reading-test/2013/12/02/2e510f26-5b92-11e3-a49b-90a0e156254b_story.html.

[6] Broach, Ann. "Bill Gates to Congress: Let us hire more foreigners." CNET Magazine," March 12, 2008, accessed on 8/8/14, http://www.cnet.com/news/bill-gates-to-congress-let-us-hire-more-foreigners/.

[7] Dickson, Paul. Sputnik: The Shock of the Century. Google Books. Accessed March 19, 2015. http://books.google.com/books?id=ZhgFUyCOhHcC&printsec=frontcover#v=onepage&q&f=false.

[8] "Sputnik Biographies—Wernher Von Braun (1912–1977)." Sputnik Biographies—Wernher Von Braun (1912–1977). Accessed August 28, 2016. http://history.nasa.gov/sputnik/braun.html.

[9] Encyclopedia Astronautica, s.v. "Von Braun." Accessed March 2, 2015. http://www.astronautix.com/astros/vonbraun.htm.

[10] "Germany Conducts First Successful V-2 Rocket Test." This Day in History. History.com. Accessed March 2, 2015. http://www.history.com/this-day-in-history/germany-conducts-first-successful-v-2-rocket-test.

[11] Marshal Space Flight Center. "Dr. Werner von Braun First Center Director, July 1 1960–Jan.27, 1970." MFSC History Office. NASA. http://history.msfc.nasa.gov/vonbraun/bio.html. Accessed 8/8/14.

[12] Zezima, Katie. "Despite Sanctions, Russia is getting a $457.9M check from NASA." The Washington Post. April 18, 2014. Accessed August 11, 2014. http://www.washingtonpost.com/blogs/post-politics/wp/2014/04/18/despite-sanctions-russia-is-getting-a-457-9m-check-from-nasa/.

[13] USA Today. August 5, 2015. Accessed August 11, 2016. http://www.usatoday.com/staff/984/ledyard-king/.

[14] "Manhattan Project." History. Atomic Heritage Foundation. Accessed February 18, 2015. http://www.mphpa.org/classic/HICC/HICC_HF3.htm.

[15] Shurkin, Joel. "Edward Teller, 'Father of the Hydrogen Bomb,' Is Dead at 95." Stanford Report. Stanford University. September 24, 2003. Accessed February 18, 2015. http://news.stanford.edu/news/2003/september24/tellerobit-924.

[16] "B-2 Spirit Stealth Bomber—Centerpiece of Long Range Strike." Northrop Grumman. Accessed June 20, 2015. http://www.northropgrumman.com/capabilities/b2spiritbomber/pages/default.aspx.

[17] Dunk, Marcus. "Hitler's Stealth Bomber: How the Nazis Were First to Design a Plane to Beat Radar." Daily Mail Online. July 8, 2009. Accessed May 3, 2015. http://www.dailymail.co.uk/news/article-1198112/Sleek-swift-deadly--Hitlers-stealth-bomber-turned-tide-Britain.html.

[18] Rostec Corporation. "Stealth Technology: Theory and Practice." Stealth Technology: Theory and Practice. September 26, 2014. Accessed May 3, 2015. http://www.defense-aerospace.com/articles-view/feature/5/157481/aircraft-stealth:-the-view-from-russia.html.

[19] Overbye, Dennis. "American and 2 Japanese Physicists Share Nobel for Work on LED Lights." The New York Times. October 7, 2014. Accessed March 3, 2015. http://www.nytimes.com/2014/10/08/science/isamu-akasaki-hiroshi-amano-and-shuji-nakamura-awarded-the-nobel-prize-in-physics.html?_r=0.

[20] Hess, Rick. "Straight Up Conversation: Common Core Guru Jason Zimba." Education Week. February 11, 2013. Accessed March 3, 2015. http://blogs.edweek.org/edweek/rick_hess_straight_up/2013/02/rhsu_straight_up_conversation_sap_honcho_jason_zimba.html.

[21] "Reactions to Sputnik—Boundless Open Textbook." Boundless. Accessed March 3, 2015. https://www.boundless.com/u-s-history/textbooks/boundless-u-s-history-textbook/the-politics-and-culture-of-abundance-1943-1960-28/the-policy-of-containment-217/reactions-to-sputnik-1209-1767/.

[22] Ibid.

[23] "World's Largest Super Collider: Abandoned." Sometimes Interesting. January 31, 2012. Accessed March 3, 2015. http://sometimes-interesting.com/2012/01/31/worlds-largest-super-collider-abandoned/.

[24] McNatt, Glenn. "Supercollider: The Particles Will Stay Undiscovered." Baltimore Sun. March 5, 1994. Accessed March 3, 2015. http://articles.baltimoresun.com/keyword/supercollider.

[25] Quirk, Trevor. "How Texas Lost the World's Largest Super Collider." Texas Monthly. How Texas Lost the World's Largest Super Collider. October 21, 2013. Accessed August 15, 2014. http://www.texasmonthly.com/story/how-texas-lost-worlds-largest-super-collider?fullpage=1.

[26] "The Metric System in the U.S." Event-Based Science Institute. Accessed October 22, 2014. http://www.ebsinstitute.com/OtherActivities/EBS.qs2df2.html.

[27] "Richard Phillips Feynman." School of Mathematics and Statistics, University of St. Andrews, Scotland. August, 2002. Accessed March 21, 2015. http://www-history.mcs.st-and.ac.uk/Biographies/Feynman.html.

[28] "RateMyProfessors.com—Find and Rate Your Professor or Campus." Rate My Professors. Accessed March 3, 2015. http://www.ratemyprofessors.com.

[29] "About PISA—OECD." About PISA—OECD. Accessed March 26, 2015. http://www.oecd.org/pisa/aboutpisa/.

[30] Strauss, Valerie. "Key PISA Test Results for U.S. Students." Washington Post. December 3, 2013. Accessed March 3, 2015. http://www.washingtonpost.com/blogs/answer-sheet/wp/2013/12/03/key-pisa-test-results-for-u-s-students/.

[31] Ibid.

[32] "What Country Spends the Most on Education?" Investopedia. February 9, 2015. Accessed March 4, 2015. http://www.investopedia.com/ask/answers/020915/what-country-spends-most-education.asp.

[33] "America's Pressing Challenge—Building a Stronger Foundation." Nsf.gov. February 1, 2006. Accessed March 4, 2015. http://www.nsf.gov/statistics/nsb0602/.

[34] "Ohio STEM Learning Network Receives Investment to Launch Science, Technology, Engineering, and Mathematics Initiative." Bill & Melinda Gates Foundation. January 1, 2014. Accessed September 19, 2015. http://www.gatesfoundation.org/Media-Center/Press-Releases/2008/01/Ohio-STEM-Learning-Network.

[35] "Foundations for Success—The Final Report of the National Mathematics Advisory Panel." US Department of Education. March 1, 2008. Accessed April 8, 2015. http://www2.ed.gov/about/bdscomm/list/mathpanel/report/final-report.pdf.

[36] Ibid.

[37] Ibid.

[38] Ibid.

[39] Ibid.

[40] "Appendix G :: Weights and Measures." Central Intelligence Agency. Accessed March 4, 2015. https://www.cia.gov/library/publications/the-world-factbook/appendix/appendix-g.html.

[41] NMAP Report, (p 54). Accessed February 19, 2015. http://www2.ed.gov/about/bdscomm/list/mathpanel/report/final-report.pdf.

[42] "George Washington." Bio.com. Accessed June 23, 2015. http://www.biography.com/people/george-washington-9524786.

[43] MailOnline, John. "Plans Unveiled for New £144bn High-speed Rail Link from Moscow to Beijing That Could Cut Trans-Siberian Journey Time by 4 DAYS." Mail Online. October 17, 2014. Accessed March 4, 2015. http://www.dailymail.co.uk/travel/travel_news/article-2796861/plans-unveiled-new-144bn-high-speed-rail-link-moscow-beijing-cut-trans-siberian-journey-time-4-hours.html.

[44] Tharoor, Ishaan. "China May Build an Undersea Train to America." The Washington Post, May 10, 2014. Accessed February 19, 2015. http://www.highbeam.com/doc/1P2-36031690.html.

[45] Discovery File, "The Metric System in the US." http://www.ebsinstitute.com/OtherActivities/EBS.qs2df2.html. Accessed 2/19/2014.

[46] Ibid.

[47] Ibid.

48 Ibid.

49 Ibid

50 Ibid

51 Ibid.

52 Ibid.

53 "The United States and the Metric System." Toward a Metric America. National Institute of Standards and Technology. October 1997. Accessed 2/19/2015. http://www.nist.gov/pml/wmd/metric/upload/1136a.pdf . Accessed 2/19/2015.

54 "Nasa's Metric Confusion Caused Mars Orbiter Loss." CNN. September 30, 1999. Accessed February 19, 2015. http://www.cnn.com/TECH/space/9909/30/mars.metric/.

55 "Arithmetic," as described in The Merriam Webster's Collegiate Dictionary, tenth Edition.

56 "Elementary Math Programs." Russian School of Mathematics. Accessed February 20, 2015. http://www.russianschool.com/our-programs/elementary-school.

57 Miller, Charles, Vern Heeren, and John Hornsby. "Basic Concepts of Set Theory." In Mathematical Ideas, 50. 10th ed. New York: Pearson, 2004.

58 Ibid (p50).

59 Stapel, Elizabeth. "Introduction to the X,y-Plane (The "Cartesian" Plane). Accessed February 20, 2015. http://www.purplemath.com/modules/plane.htm.

60 "The History of Calculus." The University of Iowa. Accessed February 20, 2015. http://www.uiowa.edu/~c22m025c/history.html.

61 The history of Zero is quite interesting. You can learn more about it: http://www.mathmojo.com/interestinglessons/originofzero/originofzero.html. (Accessed 2/20/2014).

62 It should be noted that there are numbers between the whole numbers that cannot be written as fractions. These are the irrational numbers.

63 Division by zero is not allowed in Mathematics. When a number is divided by zero, the result is called "undefined." See more at: http://www.mathmojo.com/interestinglessons/divisionl (Accessed 2/20/2014).

64 Smoller, Laura. "The Amazing History of Pi." UALR. Accessed March 4, 2015. http://ualr.edu/lasmoller/pi.html.

65 "One Billion Digits of Pi. Massachusetts Institute of Technology. Accessed March 4, 2015. https://stuff.mit.edu/afs/sipb/contrib/pi/.

66 Beginning in the 1970s, the New York City School System changed the name of head of each department from "Chairman of the Department" to "Assistant Principal Supervision" followed by the name of the department. Hence the head of the English department would be referred to as the Assistant Principal Supervision, English.

67 Hagan, Sarah. "Teaching Integer Operations with the Integer Operations Work Mat, Colored Counters, and Number Line." Math=Love. Accessed March 4, 2015. http://mathequalslove.blogspot.com/2012/08/teaching-integer-operations-with.html.

68 "What Do We Know about the Teaching and Learning of Algebra in the Elementary Grades?" http://www.nctm.org/news/content.aspx?id=12326. Accessed 8/12/2014.

[69] "Russian School of Mathematics." Russian School of Mathematics. Accessed March 4, 2015. http://www.russianschool.com/.

[70] "The Ontario Curriculum, Grade 11 and 12." Ministry of Education, Ontario. Accessed March 4, 2015. http://www.edu.gov.on.ca/eng/curriculum/secondary/math1112currb.pdf.

[71] "Common State Standards for Mathematics": http://www.corestandards.org/wp-content/uploads/Math_Standards.pdf, (accessed 9/14/2014).

[72] Ibid.

[73] The Fahrenheit readings have been rounded off to the nearest integer.

[74] "What Is the History of the Fahrenheit Scale?" WiseGEEK. Conjecture Corporation. Accessed February 21, 2015. http://www.wisegeek.org/what-is-the-history-of-the-fahrenheit-scale.htm#. slideshow.

[75] Bellis, Mary. "History of the Thermometer." About.com. Accessed September 17, 2014. Http://inventors.about.com/od/cstartinventors/a/Anders_Celsius.htm.

[76] "Anders Celsius." Super Scientists. California Energy Commission. Accessed February 21, 2015. http://energyquest.ca.gov/scientists/celsius.html.

[77] Seife, Charles. "Chapter 0." In Zero: The Biography of a Dangerous Idea. New York: Viking, 2000.

[78] Ibid.

[79] Ibid.

[80] My Expression

[81] "Give Me the Child until He Is Seven and I'll Give You the Man." Confused at a Higher Level. January 2, 2010. Accessed July 26, 2015. https://arjendu.wordpress.com/2010/01/02/give-me-the-child-until-he-is-seven-and-ill-give-you-the-man/.

[82] O'Neil, Dennis. "Learning Language." Accessed February 16, 2015. http://anthro.palomar.edu/language/language_4.htm.

[83] Rubera, Jenn. "No More Drill and Kill Teaching Basic Facts." —R.I.C. Publications. Accessed February 21, 2015. http://www.ricgroup.com.au/primary/no-more-drill-and-kill-teaching-basic-facts/.

[84] This is from the PDF version of the Canadian mathematics curriculum: http://www.edu.gov.on.ca/eng/curriculum/elementary/math18curr.pdf. Accessed August 13, 2014.

[85] Ibid.

[86] Ibid.

[87] Michael D. Lemonik, "Pluto and Beyond," Scientific American 311 (November 2014): 46-53. Accessed February 21, 2015.

[88] "The United States and the Metric System." Toward a Metric America. National Institute of Standards and Technology. http://www.nist.gov/pml/wmd/metric/upload/1136a.pdf. Accessed August 8, 2014.

[89] Ibid.

[90] Ibid.

[91] Ibid.

[92] Woolley, John, and Gerhard Peters. "Gerald Ford." The American Presidency Project. December 27, 1975. Accessed August 18, 2014. http://www.presidency.ucsb.edu/ws/?pid=5454.

[93] Ibid.

[94] Ibid.

[95] Ibid.

[96] Klein, Gill. "Half Gallon, Liters: Confusion at Gas Pump." The Christian Science Monitor. January 22, 1980. Accessed July 19, 2014. http://www.csmonitor.com/1980/0122/012204.html.

[97] Condon, Erin. "Still a Matter of Inches." Questia. September 24, 2001. Accessed February 22, 2015. https://www.questia.com/read/1G1-78790466/still-a-matter-of-inches.

[98] "Federal Role in Education." Federal Role in Education. US Department of Education. February 13, 2012. Accessed March 25, 2015. https://www2.ed.gov/about/overview/fed/role.html.

[99] "H.R. 4848 (100th): Omnibus Trade and Competitiveness Act of 1988." Govtrack.us. Accessed February 15, 2015. https://www.govtrack.us/congress/bills/100/hr4848.

[100] Ibid.

[101] "Digital Television." FCC Encyclopedia. Federal Communications Commission. Accessed April 18, 2015. http://www.fcc.gov/digital-television.

[102] Archibold, Randal. "A Spelling Champion for All Jamaicans; 12-Year-Old From Kingston Is a Hero for Winning in Washington." The New York Times. May 29, 1998. Accessed February 22, 2015. http://www.nytimes.com/1998/05/30/nyregion/spelling-champion-for-all-jamaicans-12-year-old-kingston-hero-for-winning.html,

[103] Strauss, Valerie. "Everything You Need to Know about Common Core— Ravitch." The Washington Post. January 18, 2014. Accessed July 21, 2014. http://www.washingtonpost.com/blogs/answer-sheet/wp/2014/01/18/everything-you-need-to-know-about-common-core-ravitch/.

[104] Simon, Stephanie. "New York Teachers Turn on Common Core." Politico. January 6, 2014. Accessed April 19, 2014. http://www.politico.com/story/2014/01/new-york-common-core-teachers-schools-education-102614.html#ixzz2vkZBMjNz.

[105] Rubenkam, Michael. "2 2=What? Parents Rail Against Common Core Math." NBC Washington. Accessed February 23, 2015. http://www.nbcwashington.com/news/local/22What-Parents-Rail-Against-Common-Core-Math-259363861.html.

[106] Layton, Lindsey. "Some States Rebrand Controversial Common Core Education Standards." Washington Post. January 30, 2014. Accessed February 20, 2015. http://www.washingtonpost.com/local/education/some-states-rebrand-controversial-common-core-education-standards/2014/01/30/a235843e-7ef7-11e3-9556-4a4bf7bcbd84_story.html.

[107] "About Diane." Diane Ravitch. Accessed August 16, 2015. http://dianeravitch.com/about-diane/

[108] This was an excerpt from a speech give by Diane Ravitch: http://www.washingtonpost.com/blogs/answer-sheet/wp/2014/01/18/everything-you-need-to-know-about-common-core-ravitch/.

[109] http://nces.ed.gov/pubs2011/2011004.pdf.

[110] Ibid.

[111] Ibid.

[112] Simon, Stephanie. "Special Report: Class Struggle." Reuters. February 15, 2013. Accessed March 13, 2015. http://www.reuters.com/article/2013/02/15/us-usa-charters-admissions-idUSBRE91E0HF20130215.

[113] Strauss, Valerie. "Everything You Need to Know about Common Core— Ravitch." Washington Post. January 18, 2014. Accessed August 11, 2015. http://www.washingtonpost.com/blogs/answer-sheet/wp/2014/01/18/everything-you-need-to-know-about-common-core-ravitch/.

[114] Ibid.

[115] Strauss, Valerie. "A Ridiculous Common Core Test for First Graders." Washington Post. October 21, 2013. Accessed August 24, 2015. http://www.washingtonpost.com/blogs/answer-sheet/wp/2013/10/31/a-ridiculous-common-core-test-for-first-graders/.

[116] Ibid.

[117] Ibid.

[118] Strauss, Valerie. "Everything You Need to Know about Common Core— Ravitch." Washington Post. January 18, 2014. Accessed August 11, 2015. http://www.washingtonpost.com/blogs/answer-sheet/wp/2014/01/18/everything-you-need-to-know-about-common-core-ravitch/.

[119] Ibid.

[120] "Achieve the Core." Achievethecore.org. Accessed April 4, 2015. http://achievethecore.org/about-us.

[121] Nemetz, David. "The Inside Story of the Wendy's 'Where's the Beef?' Ad, 30 Years Later." The Inside Story of the Wendy's 'Where's the Beef?' Ad, 30 Years Later. Accessed March 15, 2015. https://www.yahoo.com/tv/bp/inside-story-wendy-where-beef-ad-30-years-004259251.html.

[122] Strauss, Valerie. "Arne Duncan: 'White Suburban Moms' Upset That Common Core Shows Their Kids Aren't 'brilliant'." Washington Post. November 16, 2013. Accessed March 15, 2015. http://www.washingtonpost.com/blogs/answer-sheet/wp/2013/11/16/arne-duncan-white-surburban-moms-upset-that-common-core-shows-their-kids-arent-brilliant/.

[123] "Achieve the Core." Achievethecore.org. Accessed March 15, 2015. http://achievethecore.org/about-us.

[124] Ravitch, Diane. "The Disturbing Connection between David Coleman and Michelle Rhee." Diane Ravitchs Blog. May 30, 2012. Accessed March 13, 2015. http://dianeravitch.net/2012/05/30/the-disturbing-connection-between-david-coleman-and-michelle-rhee/.

[125] Strauss, Valerie. "What Michelle Rhee Did in D.C.: Point by Point." The Washington Post. November 2, 2010. Accessed March 13, 2015. http://voices.washingtonpost.com/answer-sheet/dc-schools/rhees-legacy-point-by-point.html.

[126] Lemann, Nicholas. "How Michelle Rhee Misled Education Reform." New Republic. May 20, 2013. Accessed March 15, 2015. http://www.newrepublic.com/article/113096/how-michelle-rhee-misled-education-reform.

[127] Baye, Rachel. "Why Michelle Rhee Is Giving Millions to Conservatives in Dozens of States." States. March 7, 2014. Accessed March 13, 2015. http://www.slate.com/articles/news_and_politics/politics/2014/03/michelle_rhee_s_studentsfirst_education_policy_is_becoming_a_new_source.html.

[128] Ibid.

[129] Strauss, Valerie. "What Michelle Rhee Did in D.C.: Point by Point." The Washington Post. November 2, 2010. Accessed March 13, 2015. http://voices.washingtonpost.com/answer-sheet/dc-schools/rhees-legacy-point-by-point.html.

[130] Ravitch, Diane. "The Disturbing Connection between David Coleman and Michelle Rhee." Diane Ravitchs Blog. May 30, 2012. Accessed March 13, 2015. http://dianeravitch.net/2012/05/30/the-disturbing-connection-between-david-coleman-and-michelle-rhee/.

[131] Strauss, Valerie. "Michelle Rhee to Step down as StudentsFirst Chief, Take 'next Step in Life'." Washington Post. August 20, 2014. Accessed March 13, 2015. http://www.washingtonpost.com/blogs/answer-sheet/wp/2014/08/13/michelle-rhee-reported-to-be-stepping-down-as-studentsfirst-chief/.

[132] Ibid.

[133] Lewin, Tamar. "Backer of Common Core School Curriculum Is Chosen to Lead College Board." The New York Times. May 15, 2012. Accessed March 15, 2015. http://www.nytimes.com/2012/05/16/education/david-coleman-to-lead-college-board.html?_r=0.

[134] Ibid.

[135] Ibid.

[136] Wiersma, William. "Individually Guided Education: An Alternative Form of Schooling." ERIC. Accessed July 18, 2014. http://eric.ed.gov/?id=ED274421.

[137] Kim, Pyeong-gook. "The Rise and Fall of Individually Guided Education 1969–1979." ERIC. Accessed April 20, 2014. http://eric.ed.gov/?id=ED465214.

[138] Winerip, Michael. "10 Years of Assessing Students With Scientific Exactitude." The New York Times. December 18, 2011. Accessed April 18, 2014. http://www.nytimes.com/2011/12/19/education/new-york-city-student-testing-over-the-past-decade.html?pagewanted=all&_r=1&.

[139] Otterman, Sharon. "Charter Founder Is Named Education Commissioner." The New York Times. May 16, 2011. Accessed February 24, 2015. http://www.nytimes.com/2011/05/17/nyregion/new-york-names-new-state-education-commissioner.html?_r=0.

[140] Taylor, Kate. "New York State Education Commissioner to Leave for Federal Post." The New York Times. December 10, 2014. Accessed February 24, 2015. http://www.nytimes.com/2014/12/11/nyregion/john-king-new-york-state-education-commissioner-is-leaving-for-federal-post.html?_r=0.

[141] Taylor, Kate. "New York State Education Commissioner to Leave for Federal Post." The New York Times. December 10, 2014. Accessed February 24, 2015. http://www.nytimes.com/2014/12/11/nyregion/john-king-new-york-state-education-commissioner-is-leaving-for-federal-post.html.

[142] Ibid.

[143] John King's curriculum vitae: http://usny.nysed.gov/about/commissioner_king.html. Accessed February 24, 2015.

[144] Otterman, Sharon. "Charter Founder Is Named Education Commissioner." The New York Times. May 16, 2011. Accessed February 24, 2015. http://www.nytimes.com/2011/05/17/nyregion/new-york-names-new-state-education-commissioner.html?_r=1&.

[145] Press Releases | Uncommon Schools. Accessed February 24, 2015. http://www.uncommonschools.org/news/press-release.

[146] Stanford, Jason. "Wall Street Behind Charter School Push." The Huffington Post. March 17, 2013. Accessed February 24, 2015. http://www.huffingtonpost.com/jason-stanford/wall-street-charter-schools_b_2467608.html.

[147] "Emotions High At Common Core Forums On Long Island." CBS New York. November 13, 2013. Accessed February 24, 2015. http://newyork.cbslocal.com/2013/11/13/emotions-high-at-common-core-forum-on-long-island/.

[148] Ibid.

[149] Gojak, Linda M. "A Reflection on 25 Years in Mathematics Education." National Council of Teachers of Mathematics. April 1, 2014. Accessed September 19, 2014. http://www.nctm.org/News-and-Calendar/Messages-from-the-President/Archive/Linda-M_-Gojak/A-Reflection-on-25-Years-in-Mathematics-Education/.

[150] Kepner, Henry (Hank). "Measure for Measure." National Council of Teachers of Mathematics. June 1, 2009. Accessed February 26, 2015. http://www.nctm.org/News-and-Calendar/Messages-from-the-President/Archive/Henry-(Hank)-Kepner,-Jr/Measure-for-Measure/.

[151] Ibid.

[152] http://www.nctm.org/about/content.aspx?id=25186. Accessed June 1, 2014.

[153] Ibid.

[154] Ibid.

[155] Ibid.

[156] "A Quote by Richard P. Feynman." Goodreads. Accessed April 8, 2015. http://www.goodreads.com/quotes/641349-i-was-terrible-in-english-i-couldn-t-stand-the-subject.

[157] http://www.nctm.org/about/content.aspx?id=25186. Accessed June 1, 2014.

[158] Ibid.

[159] "4 Steps to Problem Solving." Scholastic. (Adapted from Science World, November 5, 1993) Accessed February 20, 2015. http://teacher.scholastic.com/lessonrepro/lessonplans/steppro.htm.

[160] Ibid.

[161] "Code Breaking." HISTORY. AETN UK. April 2, 2014. Accessed February 24, 2015. http://www.history.co.uk/study-topics/history-of-ww2/code-breaking.

[162] Ibid.

[163] Ibid.

[164] Carr, Sarah. "Teachers Feel Urgency of Common Core Standards." The Advocate. September 4, 2013. Accessed January 22, 2015. http://theadvocate.com/home/6914390-125/common-core.

[165] Ibid.

[166] "Jason Zimba Interacts with Dr. Sandra Stotsky." Youtube video, 1:17, posted by No to Common Core. October 2, 2013, https://www.youtube.com/watch?v=eJZY4mh2rt8.

[167] APPENDIX 1: Finnish National Curriculum for Mathematics. Plymouth University. http://www.cimt.plymouth.ac.uk/politeia/mathematics/finland.pdf.

[168] TYRRELL, JOIE. "248 LI Principals Join Protest against Over-testing—Newsday." Newsday. January 1, 2013. Accessed November 16, 2015. http://www.newsday.com/long-island/suffolk/248-li-principals-join-protest-against-over-testing-1.6449414.

[169] Ibid.

[170] Strauss, Valerie. "A Ridiculous Common Core Test for First Graders." Washington Post. October 21, 2013. Accessed February 28, 2015. http://www.washingtonpost.com/blogs/answer-sheet/wp/2013/10/31/a-ridiculous-common-core-test-for-first-graders/.

[171] Ibid.

[172] Ibid.

[173] Ibid.

[174] Torres, Alec. "The Ten Dumbest Common Core Problems, by Alec Torres, National Review." National Review Online. March 20, 2014. Accessed February 28, 2015. http://www.nationalreview.com/article/373840/ten-dumbest-common-core-problems-alec-torres.

[175] Ibid.

[176] Strauss, Valerie. "A Ridiculous Common Core Test for First Graders." Washington Post. October 21, 2013. Accessed February 28, 2015. http://www.washingtonpost.com/blogs/answer-sheet/wp/2013/10/31/a-ridiculous-common-core-test-for-first-graders/.

[177] Ibid.

[178] Strauss, Valerie. "Gov. Cuomo Seeks Changes to 'flawed' Common Core Implementation." Washington Post. January 22, 2014. Accessed February 28, 2015. http://www.washingtonpost.com/blogs/answer-sheet/wp/2014/01/22/gov-cuomo-seeks-changes-to-flawed-common-core-implementation/.

[179] "A Quote by Bertrand Russell." Goodreads. Accessed March 15, 2015. http://www.goodreads.com/quotes/647862-mathematics-rightly-viewed-possesses-not-only-truth-but-supreme-beauty-a.

[180] Struss, Valerie. "Everything You Need to Know about Common Core—Ravitch." Washington Post. January 18, 2014. Accessed February 28, 2015. http://www.washingtonpost.com/blogs/answer-sheet/wp/2014/01/18/everything-you-need-to-know-about-common-core-ravitch/.

[181] Karen, comment on Annie Murphy Paul. "Why Parenting Is More Important than Schools." Time. October 24, 2012. Accessed February 28, 2015. http://ideas.time.com/2012/10/24/the-single-largest-advantage-parents-can-give-their-kids/.

[182] Ibid.

[183] "Bill Gates Asks Congress to Act Now to Maintain U.S. Innovation Lead." News Center. Microsoft. March 12, 2008. Accessed February 28, 2015. http://news.microsoft.com/2008/03/12/bill-gates-asks-congress-to-act-now-to-maintain-u-s-innovation-lead/.

[184] Associated Press. "US Students Lag Behind in Math & Science 2004." AYA Educational Institute. November 27, 2009. Accessed March 2, 2015. http://www.ayanetwork.com/education/index.php?option=com_content&view=article&id=93:us-students-lag-behind-in-math-a-science-2004-&catid=1:latest-news&Itemid=50.

[185] Another of Exxon's "Let's Solve This," Commercials: https://www.youtube.com/watch?v=0-R1ehkhb1I.

[186] "US High School Had the Most Nobel Prize Winners." College Confidential. Accessed March 31, 2015. http://talk.collegeconfidential.com/prep-school-admissions/1428860-us-high-school-had-the-most-nobel-prize-winners.html.

[187] "Jaime Escalante Math Program." The Futures Channel Educational Videos and Activities. Accessed March 31, 2015. http://thefutureschannel.com/jaime-escalante-math-program/.

[188] Santana, Alfredo. "Jaime Escalante." Pasadena City College. Accessed March 31, 2015. http://www.pasadena.edu/about/history/alumni/escalante/escalante.cfm.

[189] Reagan, Ronald. "Remarks to the Finalists in the Teacher in Space Project." Online by Gerhard Peters and John T. Woolley, The American Presidency Project. June 26, 1985. Accessed March 1, 2015. http://www.presidency.ucsb.edu/ws/?pid=38825.

[190] Dr. Wernher von Braun First Center Director, July 1, 1960–Jan. 27, 1970." Biography of Wernher Von Braun. Marshall Space Flight Center. Accessed March 1, 2015. http://history.msfc.nasa.gov/vonbraun/bio.html

[191] Hudson, Judith. "How and When Should I Teach My Child Her Numbers? | BabyCenter." BabyCenter. Accessed March 2, 2015. http://www.babycenter.com/404_how-and-when-should-i-teach-my-child-her-numbers_6899.bc.

[192] Ibid.

[193] "The First Tee Trustee Arnold Palmer PSA." YouTube video, :32, posted by The First Tee. May 7, 2012. Accessed February 28, 2015. https://www.youtube.com/watch?v=K8AG1UE0cEE.

[194] "PSA: Rickie Fowler Supports The First Tee." YouTube video,:30, posted by The First Tee. December 20, 2012. Accessed February 28, 2015. https://www.youtube.com/watch?v=J2aQzVz6NJI.

[195] "Learn about the Mickelson ExxonMobil Teachers Academy." ExxonMobil. Accessed February 28, 2015. http://corporate.exxonmobil.com/en/community/math-and-science/mickelson-exxonmobil-teachers-academy.

[196] "Learning Styles." —Helping Children Succeed in School. University of Illinois Extension. Accessed August 16, 2015. http://extension.illinois.edu/succeed/learningstyles.cfm

[197] Ibid.

INDEX

178, 180
lobbyists 16, 177, 193, 199
Los Angeles 197

M

Manhattan Project 13, 19, 236
Mars 11, 45, 238
Martian atmosphere 45
Massachusetts 148, 160, 238
mass of a proton 98, 99
master's degree 148, 194
mathematics
 - A 140
 - B 140
 - curriculum 15, 36, 45, 47, 53, 65, 66,
  67, 71, 82, 83, 85, 140, 145, 150,
  152, 159, 160, 170, 171, 198, 219,
  239
 - education 2, 18, 28, 41, 42, 43, 45, 47,
  65, 70, 83, 87, 89, 134, 147, 148,
  150, 152, 165, 168, 169, 171, 192,
  195
 - teacher(s) 5, 7, 19, 32, 34, 51, 60, 61,
  62, 69, 75, 77, 84, 140, 141, 152,
  154, 155, 165, 170, 178, 194, 195,
  196, 197, 198, 207
 - textbook(s) 117, 178, 227
Math Equals Love 61
Maurice Stans 112, 113, 115, 169, 193
Max
 - Born 202
 - Planck 202
measuring jars 178
megabytes 93
memorization 41, 211, 212, 213
meter(s) 39, 40, 41, 43, 90, 91, 92, 96,
  100, 101, 103, 105, 108, 117, 178,
  179, 180
meter stick 178, 180
Metric
 - Board 44, 109, 110, 111, 112, 114
 - (Conversion) Act of 1975 18, 44, 109,

110, 114, 193, 235
 - measurements 107, 119
 - system 7, 8, 13, 15, 18, 19, 20, 35, 36,
  38, 41, 42, 43, 44, 45, 47, 52, 56,
  60, 61, 63, 75, 82, 89, 90, 91, 92,
  93, 95, 99, 100, 102, 103, 105, 107,
  108, 109, 110, 112, 114, 115, 116,
  117, 118, 120, 121, 152, 157, 158,
  169, 177, 178, 191, 192, 193, 201,
  202, 203
 - trundle wheel 178
 - units 42, 44, 97, 109, 152, 178, 201
metrication chart 36
Michael D. Lemonick 89
Michelle Rhee 135, 136, 137, 138, 139,
  241, 242
Mickelson ExxonMobil Teachers Academy 245
micrometer 178
Microsoft 5, 8, 27, 192, 244
milliliter(s) 39, 91, 101, 108, 119
millimeter(s) 90, 92, 105, 178, 180
Modern Language Association 128
multiples 40, 41, 91, 93, 95, 100, 108, 178
multiplication 35, 36, 48, 53, 54, 64, 66,
  73, 79, 80, 85, 86, 87, 182, 210,
  211, 212, 213, 215, 226

N

NAACP 170
nanometer 117
NASA 11, 16, 45, 235
National
 - Council of Teachers of Mathematics
  32, 63, 143, 145, 151, 243
 - Institute of Standards 108, 238, 239
 - Mathematics Advisory Panel 34, 237
 - Science Foundation 26
NBC 126, 216, 240
negative integer 220, 221
Neil deGrasse Tyson 194
New Jersey 61, 148, 200

The First Tee 215, 245
thermometer 60, 71, 75, 82, 178, 180
Thomas M. Green 231
Treaty of the Meter 44, 109, 110
trigonometry 48, 64, 65, 140, 156, 170, 228
troy ounce 119
Trudi Hammel Garland 231
two-color counters 83, 186, 219, 220, 221, 222, 224, 226

Wernher Von Braun 13, 202, 235, 245
whole numbers 35, 36, 49, 53, 54, 56, 66, 79, 81, 83, 103, 230, 231, 238
winter 56, 70, 75, 76, 77, 78, 159
Wisconsin 200
World War II 11, 13, 157

X

x coordinate 50

U

Uncommon Schools 148, 243
union contracts 129
Unionized sport 200
United Kingdom 38, 44, 60
universe 66, 79, 93, 94, 99, 229
Usain Bolt 92
USCS measures 40, 41
US Customary System 7, 18, 37, 38, 177, 201
US Metric Board 44, 111, 112
USS Yorktown 72, 73

Y

Yahoo 231
yards 39, 41, 101, 102, 108, 113, 119
y coordinate 50
Youtube 186, 211, 212, 215, 226, 228, 231, 235, 244, 245

Z

zero 49, 53, 54, 56, 59, 63, 72, 73, 78, 79, 91, 93, 94, 97, 98, 118, 179, 183, 186, 197, 211, 217, 218, 221, 223, 224, 225, 230, 238

V

variable 50, 64, 218, 225
velocity 229
voucher programs 137

W

Wall Street 148, 243
Walter Mondale 133
wave functions 52
Weather Channel 70
weight 39, 41, 89, 91, 178, 179, 230
Wendy 133, 241
Werner Heisenberg 13, 202

Made in the USA
Middletown, DE
19 April 2021